EX LIBRES

For Evan,
With love.

SHAMBHALA LIBRARY

BACKWOODS
AND ALONG THE
SEASHORE

Selections from
The Maine Woods and *Cape Cod*

Henry David Thoreau

EDITED BY
PETER TURNER

SHAMBHALA
Boston & London
2004

FRONTISPIECE: Henry David Thoreau, 1854,
crayon on paper, by Samuel Worcester Rowse,
courtesy Concord Free Public Library

SHAMBHALA PUBLICATIONS, INC.
Horticultural Hall
300 Massachusetts Avenue
Boston, Massachusetts 02115

9 8 7 6 5 4 3 2 1

First Shambhala Library Edition
PRINTED IN CHINA
♾ This edition is printed on acid-free paper that meets
the American National Standards Institute z39.48 Standard.
Distributed in the United States by Random House, Inc.,
and in Canada by Random House of Canada Ltd

The Library of Congress catalogues the previous edition of this book as follows:
Thoreau, Henry David, 1817–1862.
Backwoods and along the seashore: selections from Henry David Thoreau's
Maine woods and Cape Cod /edited by Peter Turner.
p.   cm.—(Shambhala pocket classics)
ISBN 1-57062-056-3
ISBN 1-59030-158-7 (Shambhala Library)
1. Piscataquis County (Me.)—Description and travel. 2. Maine—Description
and travel. 3. Cape Cod (Mass.)—Description and travel. 4. Thoreau, Henry
David, 1817–1862—Journeys—Maine. 5. Thoreau, Henry David, 1817–1862—
Journeys—Massachusetts—Cape Cod. 6. Authors, American—19th century—
Journeys—Maine. 7. Authors, American—19th century—Journeys—Massa-
chusetts—Cape Cod. I. Turner, Peter, 1960–   . II. Thoreau, Henry David,
1817–1862. Maine woods. Selections. III. Thoreau, Henry David, 1817–1862.
Cape Cod. Selections. IV. Title. V. Series.
F27.P5T4   1995   94-32675
917.4104'3—dc20   CIP

Chaos and ancient Night, I come no spy
With purpose to explore or to disturb
the secrets of your realm, but . . .
     .   .   .   .   as my way
Lies through your spacious empire up to light.
                    —John Milton, *Paradise Lost*

CONTENTS

EDITOR'S PREFACE

> *We can never have enough of Nature. We must
> be refreshed by the sight of inexhaustible vigor,
> vast and Titanic features, the sea-coast with its
> wrecks, the wilderness with its living and decay-
> ing trees. . . . We need to witness our own limits
> transgressed.*
>
> —from WALDEN

FEW BOOKS have more unfairly dominated public perception of an author's life and work than
Walden. While the other three book-length works
Henry David Thoreau published or prepared for pub-
lication during his lifetime lack the grand purpose of
Walden, they contain passages on a par with his best
writing. Two of the works are the travelogues represented here: *The Maine Woods* and *Cape Cod*. The
lakes and woods of Maine offered fertile ground for
Thoreau's observations on nature and Native American culture, while the seashore of Cape Cod, which
in his day was a wild and sparsely populated place,
prompted some of his most sensitive reflections on
the human condition, as well as a wonderfully hu-
morous sketch, "The Wellfleet Oysterman," a classic
of American literature.

The Maine Woods and *Cape Cod* also reveal important themes that preoccupied Thoreau much of his life, themes which began to emerge after his first trip to Maine. At the end of August 1846, almost exactly midway through his stay at Walden Pond, Thoreau packed off for an excursion to climb Mount Katahdin. Whether driven by simple wanderlust or an inner urge to witness his "limits transgressed" is not clear. But Thoreau's encounter there with wild nature had a profound effect on him. Unlike the woods and ponds around Concord, Maine had, he confessed later in his journal, "such a smack of wildness about it as I had never tasted before." Hiking up the slopes of Katahdin, he left his companions behind and climbed alone, amid swirling clouds, to the summit. "The mountain seemed a vast aggregation of rocks, . . . the raw materials of a planet dropped from some unseen quarry," he wrote in *The Maine Woods*. There nature was not sunny or benevolent but like some wrathful deity guarding a temple: "Titanic, inhuman . . . She does not smile on [humankind]. . . . She seems to say sternly, why come ye here before your time? This ground is not prepared for you."

Three years later, in October 1849, Thoreau took his first trip to Cape Cod. Traveling with his friend Ellery Channing, he had planned to go by stagecoach as far up the Cape as they could, and then on foot to Provincetown. Thoreau had gone only as far as the shore south of Boston before witnessing firsthand that the ocean could be as savage a wilderness as Mount Katahdin. At Cohasset, the brig *Saint John* from Galway, Ireland, filled with several hundred immigrants, had run aground during a violent storm. A hundred and fifty people had died, and as Thoreau and Channing made their way to the shore, bodies were being identified and carted off in rough coffins. In "Shipwreck," the first chapter of *Cape Cod,* Thoreau first coolly surveys the scene of the wreck and then struggles to lend meaning to the deaths of the storm's victims. In a later chapter, he writes, echoing his thoughts while on Mount Katahdin, that the seashore "is a wild, rank place, . . . There is naked Nature,—inhumanly sincere, wasting no thought on man, nibbling at the cliffy shores where gulls wheel amid the spray."

Thoreau's Katahdin trip and this first trip to Cape Cod mark the emergence of a major theme in his life as a thinker and writer. While *Walden* and his essays on civil disobedience, slavery, and the abolitionist John Brown, question the meaning of the individual and his ideals in relation to society, Thoreau's underlying purpose in *The Maine Woods* and *Cape Cod* is more the pursuit of the answer to a question only dimly articulated: "What is nature?" or, especially, "What is man in nature?" Nature's mountaintops, backwoods, and shorelines become emblems of a sort of border ground, a boundary both external and internal between raw wildness and civilization. It was a boundary that at times left Thoreau awestruck and occasionally even repulsed him, but it also fascinated him and drew him back again and again. In all, Thoreau took three trips to the backwoods of Maine and four along the seashores of Cape Cod.*

Along with his fascination with the wilderness came a deeper appreciation for those who lived in it or on its margins: the mackerel fishermen of Provincetown, the oystermen of Wellfleet, and especially the Native Americans he encountered in Maine. Since boyhood, Thoreau had possessed a somewhat romantic fascination with Native Americans and their artifacts, which were occasionally found around Concord. His trip to Mount Katahdin grounded his interest, providing a practical context for his fascination with Native American culture. Shortly after his return from this journey, he began to read extensively about Native cultures, ultimately recording almost three thousand pages of extracts and his own comments and observations in his "Indian Notebooks."† What most excited Thoreau was the way in which Native peoples seemed to live in such inti-

---

*Thoreau's forth and last excursion to the Cape, taken from 12–22 June, was not described in *Cape Cod*.

†Richard Fleck, a Thoreau scholar who has studied the "Indian Notebooks" in depth, points out that they probably represent the largest body of knowledge on Native American thought written during the nineteenth century. See *The*

mate rapport with wilderness. It was during his canoe journey along the Allegash and East Branch of the Penobscot in 1857 that Thoreau finally met a living exemplar of this profound connection with nature: Joe Pollis, whom he had hired as a guide. Pollis, a chief man of Penobscot tribe, though familiar with white culture, had lost none of his knowledge of native wisdom, woodcraft, and lore. Pollis impressed Thoreau deeply, nurturing in him the belief that some of this harmony with wild nature might be learned—and even giving him the hope that he could attain it himself. On his return from this last trip to Maine, Thoreau confided in a letter to his friend Harrison Blake:

> Having returned, I flatter myself that the world appears in some respects a little larger, and not, as usual, smaller and shallower, for having extended my range. I have made a short excursion into the new world which the Indian dwells in, or is. He begins where we leave off. It is worth the while to detect new faculties in man,—he is so much the more divine; and anything that fairly excites our admiration expands us. The Indian, who can find his way so wonderfully in the

---

Indians of Thoreau: Selections from the Indian Notebooks, edited by Richard F. Fleck (Albuquerque: Hummingbird Press, 1974), p. 3.

woods, possess so much intelligence which the white man does not,—and it increases my own capacity as well as faith to observe it. I rejoice to find that intelligence flows in other channels than I know. It redeems for me portions of what seemed brutish before. . . . It is a great satisfaction to find that your oldest convictions are permanent. With regard to essentials, I have never had occasion to change my mind. The aspect of the world varies from year to year as the landscape is differently clothed, but I find that the *truth* is still *true*, and I never regret any emphasis which it may have inspired. Ktaadn is there still, but much more surely my old conviction is there, resting with more than mountain breadth and weight on the world, the source still fertilizing streams, and affording glorious views from its summit if I can get up to it again.

Peter Turner
Cambridge, Mass.
August 1994

A NOTE ON THE TEXTS

The Maine Woods consists of edited versions of three long essays: "Ktaadn and the Maine Woods," which originally appeared serially in the *Union Magazine*, July–November 1848; "Chesuncook," which appeared serially in the *Atlantic Monthly,* June–August 1858; a previously unpublished essay, "The Allegash and the East Branch"; and an appendix of technical terms. These were edited by Thoreau's sister Sophia and his traveling companion and friend Ellery Channing and published posthumously as *The Maine Woods* by Ticknor and Fields in 1864.

Versions of four chapters of *Cape Cod* were first published in *Putnum's Monthly Magazine* in June–August 1855 and later published, in edited form with six other chapters, by Ticknor and Fields in 1865.

The selections reprinted here are from the text of the 1864 edition of *The Maine Woods* and the 1865 edition of *Cape Cod.*

The Maine Woods

Ktaadn

O N T H E 31st of August, 1846, I left Concord in
Massachusetts for Bangor and the backwoods
of Maine, by way of the railroad and steamboat, intending to accompany a relative of mine engaged in
the lumber-trade in Bangor, as far as a dam on the
west branch of the Penobscot, in which property he
was interested. From this place, which is about one
hundred miles by the river above Bangor, thirty miles
from the Houlton military road, and five miles beyond the last log-hut, I proposed to make excursions
to Mount Ktaadn, the second highest mountain in
New England, about thirty miles distant, and to some
of the lakes of the Penobscot, either alone or with
such company as I might pick up there.

The next forenoon, Tuesday, September 1st, I
started with my companion in a buggy from Bangor
for "up river," expecting to be overtaken the next day
night at Mattawamkeag Point, some sixty miles off,
by two more Bangoreans, who had decided to join us
in a trip to the mountain. We had each a knapsack or
bag filled with such clothing and articles as were in-
dispensable, and my companion carried his gun.

Within a dozen miles of Bangor we passed through the villages of Stillwater and Oldtown, built at the falls of the Penobscot; which furnish the principal power by which the Maine woods are converted into lumber. The mills are built directly over and across the river. Here is a close jam, a hard rub, at all seasons; and then the once green tree, long since white, I need not say as the driven snow, but as a driven log, becomes lumber merely. Here your inch, your two and your three inch stuff begin to be, and Mr. Sawyer marks off those spaces which decide the destiny of so many prostrate forests. Through this steel riddle, more or less coarse, is the arrowy Maine forest, from Ktaadn and Chesuncook, and the head-waters of the St. John, relentlessly sifted, till it comes out boards, clapboards, laths, and shingles such as the wind can take, still perchance to be slit and slit again, till men get a size that will suit. Think how stood the white-pine tree on the shore of Chesuncook, its branches soughing with the four winds, and every individual needle trembling in the sunlight,—think how it stands with it now,—sold, perchance, to the New England Friction-Match Company!

The next morning we drove along through a high and hilly country, in view of Cold-Stream Pond, a beautiful lake four or five miles long, and came into the Houlton road again, here called the military road, at Lincoln, forty-five miles from Bangor, where there is quite a village for this country,—the principal one above Oldtown. Learning that there were several wigwams here, on one of the Indian islands, we left our horse and wagon, and walked through the forest half a mile to the river, to procure a guide to the mountain. It was not till after considerable search that we discovered their habitations,—small huts, in a retired place, where the scenery was unusually soft and beautiful, and the shore skirted with pleasant meadows and graceful elms. We paddled ourselves across to the island-side in a canoe, which we found on the shore. Near where we landed sat an Indian girl ten or twelve years old, on a rock in the water, in the sun, washing, and humming or moaning a song meanwhile. It was an aboriginal strain. A salmon-spear, made wholly of wood, lay on the shore, such as they might have used before white men came. It had an elastic piece of wood fastened to one side of its point, which slipped over and closed upon the fish, somewhat like the contrivance for holding a bucket at the end of a well-pole. As we walked up to the nearest house, we were met by a sally of a dozen wolfish-looking dogs, which may have been lineal descendants from the ancient Indian dogs, which the first voyageurs describe as "their wolves." I suppose they were. The occupant soon appeared, with a long pole in his hand, with which he beat off the dogs, while he parleyed with us. A stalwart, but dull and greasy-looking fellow, who told us, in his sluggish way, in answer to our questions, as if it were the first serious business he had to do that day, that there *were* Indians going "up river"—he and one other—today, before noon. And who was the other? Louis Neptune, who lives in the next house. Well, let us go over and see Louis together. The same doggish reception, and Louis Neptune makes his appearance,—a small, wiry man, with puckered and wrinkled face, yet he seemed the chief man of the two; the same, as I remembered, who had accompanied Jackson to the mountain in '37. The same questions were put to Louis, and the same information obtained, while the other Indian stood by. It appeared that they were going to start by noon, with two canoes, to go up to Chesuncook to hunt moose,—to be gone a month. "Well, Louis, suppose you get to the Point [to the Five Islands, just below Mattawamkeag], to camp, we walk on up the West Branch to-morrow,—four of us,—and wait for you at the dam, or this side. You overtake us to-morrow or next day, and take us into your canoes. We stop for you, you stop for us. We pay you for your trouble." "Ye!" replied Louis, "may be you carry some provision for all,—some pork,—some bread,—and so pay." He said, "Me sure get some moose"; and when I asked if he thought Pomola would let us go up, he answered that we must plant one bottle of rum on the top; he had planted good many; and when he looked again, the rum was all gone. He had been up two or three times: he had planted letter,—English, German, French, &c. These men were slightly clad in shirt and pantaloons, like laborers with us in warm weather. They did not invite us into their houses, but met us outside. So we left the Indians, thinking ourselves lucky to have secured such guides and companions.

About noon we reached the Mattawamkeag, fifty-six miles from Bangor by the way we had come, and put up at a frequented house still on the Houlton road, where the Houlton stage stops. Here was a substantial covered bridge over the Mattawamkeag, built, I think they said, some seventeen years before. We had dinner,—where, by the way, and even at breakfast, as well as supper, at the public-houses on this road, the front rank is composed of various kinds of "sweet cakes," in a continuous line from one end of the table to the other. I think I may safely say that there was a row of ten or a dozen plates of this kind set before us two here. To account for which, they say that, when the lumberers come out of the woods, they have a craving for cakes and pies, and such sweet things, which there are almost unknown, and this is the *supply* to satisfy that *demand*. The supply is always equal to the demand, and these hungry men think a good deal of getting their money's worth. No doubt the balance of victuals is restored by the time they reach Bangor,—Mattawamkeag takes off the raw edge. Well, over this front rank, I say, you, coming from the "sweet cake" side, with a cheap philosophic indifference though it may be, have to assault what there is behind, which I do not by any means mean to insinuate is insufficient in quantity or quality to supply that other demand, of men, not from the woods, but from the towns, for venison and strong country fare. After dinner we strolled down to the "Point," formed by the junction of the two rivers, which is said to be the scene of an ancient battle between the Eastern Indians and the Mohawks, and searched there carefully for relics, though the men at the bar-room had never heard of such things; but we found only some flakes of arrow-head stone, some points of arrow-heads, one small leaden bullet, and some colored beads, the last to be referred, perhaps, to early fur-trader days.

Early the next morning we had mounted our packs, and prepared for a tramp up the West Branch, my companion having turned his horse out to pasture for a week or ten days, thinking that a bite of fresh grass, and a taste of running water, would do him as much good as backwoods fare and new country influences his master. Leaping over a fence, we began to follow an obscure trail up the northern bank of the Penobscot. There was now no road further, the river being the only highway, and but half a dozen log-huts confined to its banks, to be met with for thirty miles. On either hand, and beyond, was a wholly uninhabited wilderness, stretching to Canada. Neither horse nor cow, nor vehicle of any kind, had ever passed over this ground; the cattle, and the few bulky articles which the loggers use, being got up in the winter on the ice, and down again before it breaks up. The evergreen woods had a decidedly sweet and bracing fragrance; the air was a sort of diet-drink, and we walked on buoyantly in Indian file, stretching our legs. Occasionally there was a small opening on the bank, made for the purpose of log-rolling, where we got a sight of the river,—always a rocky and rippling stream. The roar of the rapids, the note of a whistler-duck on the river, of the jay and chickadee around us, and of the pigeon-woodpecker in the openings, were the sounds that we heard. This was what you might call a bran-new country; the only roads were of Nature's making, and the few houses were camps. Here, then, one could no longer accuse institutions and society, but must front the true source of evil.

There are three classes of inhabitants who either frequent or inhabit the country which we had now entered;—first, the loggers, who, for a part of the year, the winter and spring, are far the most numerous, but in the summer, except a few explorers for timber, completely desert it; second, the few settlers I have named, the only permanent inhabitants, who live on the verge of it, and help raise supplies for the former; third, the hunters, mostly Indians, who range over it in their season.

We found the East Branch a large and rapid stream at its mouth, and much deeper than it appeared. Having with some difficulty discovered the trail again, we kept up the south side of the West Branch, or main river, passing by some rapids called Rock-Ebeeme, the roar of which we heard through the woods, and, shortly after, in the thickest of the wood, some empty loggers' camps, still new, which were occupied the previous winter. Though we saw a few more afterwards, I will make one account serve for all. These were such houses as the lumberers of Maine spend the winter in, in the wilderness. There were the camps and the hovels for the cattle, hardly distinguishable, except that the latter had no chimney. These camps were about twenty feet long by fifteen wide, built of logs,—hemlock, cedar, spruce, or yellow birch,—one kind alone, or all together, with the bark on; two or three large ones first, one directly above another, and notched together at the ends, to the height of three or four feet, then of smaller logs resting upon transverse ones at the ends, each of the last successively shorter than the other, to form the roof. The chimney was an oblong square hole in the middle, three or four feet in diameter, with a fence of logs as high as the ridge. The interstices were filled with moss, and the roof was shingled with long and handsome splints of cedar, or spruce, or pine, rifted with a sledge and cleaver. The fire-place, the most important place of all, was in shape and size like the chimney, and directly under it, defined by a log fence or fender on the ground, and a heap of ashes, a foot or two deep, within, with solid benches of split logs running round it. Here the fire usually melts the snow, and dries the rain before it can descend to quench it. The faded beds of arbor-vitae leaves extended under the eaves on either hand. There was the place for the water-pail, pork-barrel, and wash-basin, and generally a dingy pack of cards left on a log. Usually a good deal of whittling was expended on the latch, which was made of wood, in the form of an iron one. These houses are made comfortable by the huge fires, which can be afforded night and day.

Eighteen miles from the Point brought us in sight of McCauslin's, or "Uncle George's," as he was familiarly called by my companions, to whom he was well known, where we intended to break our long fast. His house was in the midst of an extensive clearing of intervale, at the mouth of the Little Schoodic River, on the opposite or north bank of the Penobscot. So we collected on a point of the shore, that we might be seen, and fired our gun as a signal, which brought out his dogs forthwith, and thereafter their master, who in due time took us across in his bateau. This clearing was bounded abruptly, on all sides but the river, by the naked stems of the forest, as if you were to cut only a few feet square in the midst of a thousand acres of mowing, and set down a thimble therein. He had a whole heaven and horizon to himself, and the sun seemed to be journeying over his clearing only the live-long day. Here we concluded to spend the night, and wait for the Indians, as there was no stopping-place so convenient above. He had seen no Indians pass, and this did not often happen without his knowledge. He thought that his dogs sometimes gave notice of the approach of Indians half an hour before they arrived.

McCauslin was a Kennebec man, of Scotch descent, who had been a waterman twenty-two years, and had driven on the lakes and head-waters of the Penobscot five or six springs in succession, but was now settled here to raise supplies for the lumberers and for himself. He entertained us a day or two with true Scotch hospitality, and would accept no recompense for it. A man of a dry wit and shrewdness, and a general intelligence which I had not looked for in the backwoods. In fact, the deeper you penetrate into the woods, the more intelligent, and, in one sense, less countrified do you find the inhabitants; for always the pioneer has been a traveller, and, to some extent, a man of the world; and, as the distances with which he is familiar are greater, so is his information more general and far reaching than the villager's. If I were to look for a narrow, uninformed, and countrified mind, as opposed to the intelligence and refinement which are thought to emanate from cities, it would be among the rusty inhabitants of an old-settled country, on farms all run out and gone to seed with life-everlasting, in the towns about Boston, even on the high-road in Concord, and not in the backwoods of Maine.

The next morning, the weather proving fair enough for our purpose, we prepared to start, and, the Indians having failed us, persuaded McCauslin, who was not unwilling to revisit the scenes of his driving, to accompany us in their stead, intending to engage one other boatman on the way. A strip of cotton cloth for a tent, a couple of blankets, which would suffice for the whole party, fifteen pounds of hard bread, ten pounds of "clear" pork, and a little tea, made up "Uncle George's" pack. The last three articles were calculated to be provision enough for six men for a week, with what we might pick up. A tea-kettle, a frying-pan, and an axe, to be obtained at the last house, would complete our outfit.

We were soon out of McCauslin's clearing, and in the ever green woods again. The obscure trail made by the two settlers above, which even the woodman is sometimes puzzled to discern, erelong crossed a narrow, open strip in the woods overrun with weeds, called the Burnt Land, where a fire had raged formerly, stretching northward nine or ten miles, to

Millinocket Lake. At the end of three miles, we
reached Shad Pond, or Noliseemack, an expansion
of the river. Hodge, the Assistant State Geologist,
who passed through this on the 25th of June, 1837,
says, "We pushed our boat through an acre or more of
buck-beans, which had taken root at the bottom, and
bloomed above the surface in the greatest profusion
and beauty." Thomas Fowler's house is four miles
from McCauslin's, on the shore of the pond, at the
mouth of the Millinocket River, and eight miles from
the lake of the same name, on the latter stream. This
lake affords a more direct course to Ktaadn, but we
preferred to follow the Penobscot and the Pamadumcook lakes. Fowler was just completing a new log-
hut, and was sawing out a window through the logs,
nearly two feet thick, when we arrived. He had
begun to paper his house with spruce-bark, turned
inside out, which had a good effect, and was in keeping with the circumstances. Instead of water we got
here a draught of beer, which, it was allowed, would
be better; clear and thin, but strong and stringent as
the cedar-sap. It was as if we sucked at the very teats
of Nature's pine-clad bosom in these parts,—the sap
of all Millinocket botany commingled,—the top-
most, most fantastic, and spiciest sprays of the primitive wood, and whatever invigorating and stringent
gum or essence it afforded steeped and dissolved in
it,—a lumberer's drink, which would acclimate and
naturalize a man at once,—which would make him

see green, and, if he slept, dream that he heard the wind sough among the pines. Here was a fife, praying to be played on, through which we breathed a few tuneful strains,—brought hither to tame wild beasts. As we stood upon the pile of chips by the door, fish-hawks were sailing overhead; and here, over Shad Pond, might daily be witnessed the tyranny of the bald-eagle over that bird. Tom pointed away over the lake to a bald-eagle's nest, which was plainly visible more than a mile off, on a pine, high above the surrounding forest, and was frequented from year to year by the same pair, and held sacred by him. There were these two houses only there, his low hut and the eagles' airy cart-load of fagots. Thomas Fowler, too, was persuaded to join us, for two men were necessary to manage the bateau, which was soon to be our carriage, and these men needed to be cool and skilful for the navigation of the Penobscot. Tom's pack was soon made, for he had not far to look for his waterman's boots, and a red-flannel shirt. This is the favorite color with lumbermen; and red flannel is reputed to possess some mysterious virtues, to be most healthful and convenient in respect to perspiration. In every gang there will be a large proportion of red birds. We took here a poor and leaky bateau, and began to pole up the Millinocket two miles, to the elder Fowler's, in order to avoid the Grand Falls of the Penobscot, intending to exchange our bateau there for a better.

* * *

There were six of us, including the two boatmen. With our packs heaped up near the bows, and ourselves disposed as baggage to trim the boat, with instructions not to move in case we should strike a rock, more than so many barrels of pork, we pushed out into the first rapid, a slight specimen of the stream we had to navigate. With Uncle George in the stern, and Tom in the bows, each using a spruce pole about twelve feet long, pointed with iron,* and poling on the same side, we shot up the rapids like a salmon, the water rushing and roaring around, so that only a practised eye could distinguish a safe course, or tell what was deep water and what rocks, frequently grazing the latter on one or both sides, with a hundred as narrow escapes as ever the Argo had in passing through the Symplegades. I, who had had some experience in boating, had never experienced any half so exhilarating before.

We were soon in the smooth water of the Quakish Lake, and took our turns at rowing and paddling across it. It is a small, irregular, but handsome lake, shut in on all sides by the forest, and showing no traces of man but some low boom in a distant cove, reserved for spring use. The spruce and cedar on its shores, hung with gray lichens, looked at a distance

---

*The Canadians call it *picquer de fond.*

like the ghosts of trees. Ducks were sailing here and there on its surface, and a solitary loon, like a more living wave,—a vital spot on the lake's surface,— laughed and frolicked, and showed its straight leg, for our amusement. Joe Merry Mountain appeared in the northwest, as if it were looking down on this lake especially; and we had our first, but a partial view of Ktaadn, its summit veiled in clouds, like a dark isthmus in that quarter, connecting the heavens with the earth.

It being about the full of the moon, and a warm and pleasant evening, we decided to row five miles by moonlight to the head of the North Twin Lake, lest the wind should rise on the morrow. After one mile of river, or what the boatmen call "thorough-fare,"—for the river becomes at length only the con-necting link between the lakes,—and some slight rapid which had been mostly made smooth water by the dam, we entered the North Twin Lake just after sundown, and steered across for the river "thorough-fare," four miles distant. This is a noble sheet of water, where one may get the impression which a new country and a "lake of the woods" are fitted to create. There was the smoke of no log-hut nor camp of any kind to greet us, still less was any lover of na-ture or musing traveller watching our bateau from the distant hills; not even the Indian hunter was there, for he rarely climbs them, but hugs the river

like ourselves. No face welcomed us but the fine
fantastic sprays of free and happy evergreen trees,
waving one above another in their ancient home. At
first the red clouds hung over the western shore as
gorgeously as if over a city, and the lake lay open to
the light with even a civilized aspect, as if expecting
trade and commerce, and towns and villas. We could
distinguish the inlet to the South Twin, which is said
to be the larger, where the shore was misty and blue,
and it was worth the while to look thus through a
narrow opening across the entire expanse of a concealed lake to its own yet more dim and distant
shore. The shores rose gently to ranges of low hills
covered with forests; and though, in fact, the most
valuable white pine timber, even about this lake, had
been culled out, this would never have been sus-
pected by the voyager. The impression, which indeed
corresponded with the fact, was, as if we were upon
a high table-land between the States and Canada,
the northern side of which is drained by the St. John
and Chaudiere, the southern by the Penobscot and
Kennebec. There was no bold mountainous shore, as
we might have expected, but only isolated hills and
mountains rising here and there from the plateau.
The country is an archipelago of lakes,—the lake-
country of New England. Their levels vary but a few
feet, and the boat-men, by short portages, or by none
at all, pass easily from one to another. They say that
at very high water the Penobscot and the Kennebec

flow into each other, or at any rate, that you may lie with your face in the one and your toes in the other. Even the Penobscot and St. John have been connected by a canal, so that the lumber of the Allegash, instead of going down the St. John, comes down the Penobscot; and the Indian's tradition, that the Penobscot once ran both ways for his convenience, is, in one sense, partially realized to-day.

None of our party but McCauslin had been above this lake, so we trusted to him to pilot us, and we could not but confess the importance of a pilot on these waters. While it is river, you will not easily forget which way is up stream; but when you enter a lake, the river is completely lost, and you scan the distant shores in vain to find where it comes in.

About nine o'clock we reached the river, and ran our boat into a natural haven between some rocks, and drew her out on the sand. This camping-ground McCauslin had been familiar with in his lumbering days, and he now struck it unerringly in the moonlight, and we heard the sound of the rill which would supply us with cool water emptying into the lake. The first business was to make a fire, an operation which was a little delayed by the wetness of the fuel and the ground, owing to the heavy showers of the afternoon. The fire is the main comfort of the camp, whether in summer or winter, and is about as ample at one season as at another. It is as well for cheerful-

ness as for warmth and dryness. It forms one side of
the camp; one bright side at any rate. Some were dispersed to fetch in dead trees and boughs, while
Uncle George felled the birches and beeches which
stood convenient, and soon we had a fire some ten
feet long by three or four high, which rapidly dried
the sand before it. This was calculated to burn all
night. We next proceeded to pitch our tent; which
operation was performed by sticking our two spike-
poles into the ground in a slanting direction, about
ten feet apart, for rafters, and then drawing our
cotton cloth over them, and tying it down at the
ends, leaving it open in front, shed-fashion. But this
evening the wind carried the sparks on to the tent
and burned it. So we hastily drew up the bateau just
within the edge of the woods before the fire, and
propping up one side three or four feet high, spread
the tent on the ground to lie on; and with the corner
of a blanket, or what more or less we could get to put
over us, lay down with our heads and bodies under
the boat, and our feet and legs on the sand toward
the fire. At first we lay awake, talking of our course,
and finding ourselves in so convenient a posture for
studying the heavens, with the moon and stars shining in our faces, our conversation naturally turned
upon astronomy, and we recounted by turns the most
interesting discoveries in that science. But at length
we composed ourselves seriously to sleep. It was interesting, when awakened at midnight, to watch the

grotesque and fiend-like forms and motions of some one of the party, who, not being able to sleep, had got up silently to arouse the fire, and add fresh fuel, for a change; now stealthily hugging a dead tree from out the dark, and heaving it on, now stirring up the embers with his fork, or tiptoeing about to observe the stars, watched, perchance, by half the prostrate party in breathless silence; so much the more intense because they were awake, while each supposed his neighbor sound asleep. Thus aroused, I too brought fresh fuel to the fire, and then rambled along the sandy shore in the moonlight, hoping to meet a moose, come down to drink, or else a wolf. The little rill tinkled the louder, and peopled all the wilderness for me; and the glassy smoothness of the sleeping lake, laving the shores of a new world, with the dark, fantastic rocks rising here and there from its surface, made a scene not easily described. It has left such an impression of stern, yet gentle, wildness on my memory as will not soon be effaced.

Not far from midnight we were one after another awakened by rain falling on our extremities; and as each was made aware of the fact by cold or wet, he drew a long sigh and then drew up his legs, until gradually we all had sidled round from lying at right angles with the boat, till our bodies formed an acute angle with it, and were wholly protected. When next we awoke, the moon and stars were shining again, and there were signs of dawn in the east. I have been thus particular in order to convey some idea of a night in the woods.

In the next nine miles, which were the extent of our voyage, and which it took us the rest of the day to get over, we rowed across several small lakes, poled up numerous rapids and thoroughfares, and carried over four portages.

The last half-mile carried us to the Sowadnehunk dead-water, so called from the stream of the same name, signifying "running between mountains," an important tributary which comes in a mile above. Here we decided to camp, about twenty miles from the Dam, at the mouth of Murch Brook and the Aboljacknagesic, mountain streams, broad off from Ktaadn, and about a dozen miles from its summit; having made fifteen miles this day.

We had been told by McCauslin that we should here find trout enough: so, while some prepared the camp, the rest fell to fishing. Seizing the birch-poles which some party of Indians, or white hunters, had left on the shore, and baiting our hooks with pork, and with trout, as soon as they were caught, we cast our lines into the mouth of the Aboljacknagesic, a clear, swift, shallow stream, which came in from Ktaadn. Instantly a shoal of white chivin (*Leucisci pulchelli*), silvery roaches, cousin-trout, or what not, large and small, prowling thereabouts, fell upon our bait, and one after another were landed amidst the bushes. Anon their cousins, the true trout, took their turn, and alternately the speckled trout, and the silvery roaches, swallowed the bait as fast as we could throw in; and the finest specimens of both that I have ever seen, the largest one weighing three pounds, were heaved upon the shore, though at first in vain, to wriggle down into the water again, for we stood in the boat; but soon we learned to remedy this evil: for one, who had lost his hook, stood on shore to catch them as they fell in a perfect shower around him,—sometimes, wet and slippery, full in his face and bosom, as his arms were outstretched to receive them. While yet alive, before their tints had faded, they glistened like the fairest flowers, the product of primitive rivers; and he could hardly trust his senses, as he stood over them, that these jewels should have swam away in that Aboljacknagesic water for so long, so many dark ages;—these bright fluviatile flowers, seen of Indians only, made beautiful, the Lord only knows why, to swim there! I could understand better, for this, the truth of mythology, the fables of Proteus, and all those beautiful sea-monsters,—how all history, indeed, put to a terrestrial use, is mere history; but put to a celestial, is mythology always.

But there is the rough voice of Uncle George, who commands at the frying-pan, to send over what you've got, and then you may stay till morning. The pork sizzles, and cries for fish.

* * *

In the night I dreamed of trout-fishing; and, when at length I awoke, it seemed a fable that this painted fish swam there so near my couch, and rose to our hooks the last evening, and I doubted if I had not dreamed it all. So I arose before dawn to test its truth, while my companions were still sleeping. There stood Ktaadn with distinct and cloudless outline in the moonlight; and the rippling of the rapids was the only sound to break the stillness. Standing on the shore, I once more cast my line into the stream, and found the dream to be real and the fable true. The speckled trout and silvery roach, like flying-fish, sped swiftly through the moonlight air, describing bright arcs on the dark side of Ktaadn, until moonlight, now fading into daylight, brought satiety to my mind, and the minds of my companions, who had joined me.

By six o'clock, having mounted our packs and a good blanketful of trout, ready dressed, and swung up such baggage and provision as we wished to leave behind, upon the tops of saplings, to be out of the reach of bears, we started for the summit of the mountain, distant, as Uncle George said the boat-men called it, about four miles, but as I judged, and as it proved, nearer fourteen. He had never been any nearer the mountain than this, and there was not the slightest trace of man to guide us further in this direction. At first, pushing a few rods up the Aboljacknagesic, or "open-land stream," we fastened our bateau to a tree, and travelled up the north side, through burnt lands, now partially overgrown with young aspens, and other shrubbery; but soon, re-crossing this stream, where it was about fifty or sixty feet wide, upon a jam of logs and rocks,—and you could cross it by this means almost anywhere,—we struck at once for the highest peak, over a mile or more of comparatively open land still, very gradually ascending the while. Here it fell to my lot, as the oldest mountain-climber, to take the lead. So, scanning the woody side of the mountain, which lay still at an indefinite distance, stretched out some seven or eight miles in length before us, we determined to steer directly for the base of the highest peak, leaving a large slide, by which, as I have since learned, some of our predecessors ascended, on our left. This course would lead us parallel to a dark seam in the forest, which marked the bed of a torrent, and over a slight spur, which extended southward from the main mountain, from whose bare summit we could get an outlook over the country, and climb directly up the peak, which would then be close at hand.

At length we reached an elevation sufficiently bare to afford a view of the summit, still distant and blue, almost as if retreating from us. A torrent, which proved to be the same we had crossed, was seen tumbling down in front, literally from out of the clouds.

But this glimpse at our whereabouts was soon lost, and we were buried in the woods again. The wood was chiefly yellow birch, spruce, fir, mountain-ash, or round-wood, as the Maine people call it, and moose-wood. It was the worst kind of travelling; sometimes like the densest scrub-oak patches with us. The cornel, or bunch-berries, were very abundant, as well as Solomon's seal and moose-berries. Blueberries were distributed along our whole route; and in one place the bushes were drooping with the weight of the fruit, still as fresh as ever. It was the 7th of September. Such patches afforded a grateful repast, and served to bait the tired party forward. When any lagged behind, the cry of "blueberries" was most effectual to bring them up. Even at this elevation we passed through a moose-yard, formed by a large flat rock, four or five rods square, where they tread down the snow in winter. At length, fearing that if we held the direct course to the summit, we should not find any water near our camping-ground, we gradually swerved to the west, till, at four o'clock, we struck again the torrent which I have mentioned, and here, in view of the summit, the weary party decided to camp that night.

In the morning, after whetting our appetite on some raw pork, a wafer of hard bread, and a dipper of condensed cloud or waterspout, we all together began to make our way up the falls, which I have described; this time choosing the right hand, or highest peak, which was not the one I had approached before. But soon my companions were lost to my sight behind the mountain ridge in my rear, which still seemed ever retreating before me, and I climbed alone over huge rocks, loosely poised, a mile or more, still edging toward the clouds; for though the day was clear elsewhere, the summit was concealed by mist. The mountain seemed a vast aggregation of loose rocks, as if some time it had rained rocks, and they lay as they fell on the mountain sides, nowhere fairly at rest, but leaning on each other, all rocking-stones, with cavities between, but scarcely any soil or smoother shelf. They were the raw materials of a planet dropped from an unseen quarry, which the vast chemistry of nature would anon work up, or work down, into the smiling and verdant plains and valleys of earth. This was an undone extremity of the globe; as in lignite, we see coal in the process of formation.

At length I entered within the skirts of the cloud which seemed forever drifting over the summit, and yet would never be gone, but was generated out of that pure air as fast as it flowed away; and when, a quarter of a mile farther, I reached the summit of the ridge, which those who have seen in clearer weather say is about five miles long, and contains a thousand acres of table-land, I was deep within the hostile ranks of clouds, and all objects were obscured by

them. Now the wind would blow me out a yard of
clear sunlight, wherein I stood; then a gray, dawning
light was all it could accomplish, the cloud-line ever
rising and falling with the wind's intensity. Sometimes it seemed as if the summit would be cleared in
a few moments, and smile in sunshine: but what was
gained on one side was lost on another. It was like sitting in a chimney and waiting for the smoke to blow
away. It was, in fact, a cloud-factory,—these were the
cloud-works, and the wind turned them off done
from the cool, bare rocks. Occasionally, when the
windy columns broke in to me, I caught sight of a
dark, damp crag to the right or left; the mist driving
ceaselessly between it and me. It reminded me of the
creations of the old epic and dramatic poets, of Atlas,
Vulcan, the Cyclops, and Prometheus. Such as Cau-
casus and the rock where Prometheus was bound.
Aeschylus had no doubt visited such scenery as this.
It was vast, Titanic, and such as man never inhabits.
Some part of the beholder, even some vital part,
seems to escape through the loose grating of his ribs
as he ascends. He is more lone than you can imagine.
There is less of substantial thought and fair understanding in him, than in the plains where men inhabit. His reason is dispersed and shadowy, more
thin and subtile, like the air. Vast, Titanic, inhuman
Nature has got him at disadvantage, caught him
alone, and pilfers him of some of his divine faculty.
She does not smile on him as in the plains. She

seems to say sternly, why came ye here before your time? This ground is not prepared for you. Is it not enough that I smile in the valleys? I have never made this soil for thy feet, this air for thy breathing, these rocks for thy neighbors. I cannot pity nor fondle thee here, but forever relentlessly drive thee hence to where I *am* kind. Why seek me where I have not called thee, and then complain because you find me but a step-mother! Shouldst thou freeze or starve, or shudder thy life away, here is no shrine, nor altar, nor any access to my ear.

> Chaos and ancient Night, I come no spy
> With purpose to explore or to disturb
> The secrets of your realm, but . . .
> . . . . as my way
> Lies through your spacious empire up to light.

The tops of mountains are among the unfinished parts of the globe, whither it is a slight insult to the gods to climb and pry into their secrets, and try their effect on our humanity. Only daring and insolent men, perchance, go there. Simple races, as savages, do not climb mountains,—their tops are sacred and mysterious tracts never visited by them. Pomola is always angry with those who climb to the summit of Ktaadn.

I had brought my whole pack to the top, not knowing but I should have to make my descent to the

river, and possibly to the settled portion of the State
alone, and by some other route, and wishing to have
a complete outfit with me. But at length, fearing
that my companions would be anxious to reach the
river before night, and knowing that the clouds might
rest on the mountain for days, I was compelled to
descend. Occasionally, as I came down, the wind
would blow me a vista open, through which I could
see the country eastward, boundless forests, and
lakes, and streams, gleaming in the sun, some of
them emptying into the East Branch. There were
also new mountains in sight in that direction. Now
and then some small bird of the sparrow family
would flit away before me, unable to command its
course, like a fragment of the gray rock blown off by
the wind.

I found my companions where I had left them, on
the side of the peak, gathering the mountain cranberries, which filled every crevice between the rocks,
together with blueberries, which had a spicier flavor
the higher up they grew, but were not the less agreeable to our palates. When the country is settled, and
roads are made, these cranberries will perhaps become an article of commerce. From this elevation,
just on the skirts of the clouds, we could overlook the
country, west and south, for a hundred miles. There
it was, the State of Maine, which we had seen on the
map, but not much like that,—immeasurable forest
for the sun to shine on, that eastern *stuff* we hear of

in Massachusetts. No clearing, no house. It did not look as if a solitary traveller had cut so much as a walking-stick there. Countless lakes,—Moosehead in the southwest, forty miles long by ten wide, like a gleaming silver platter at the end of the table; Chesuncook, eighteen long by three wide, without an island; Millinocket, on the south, with its hundred islands; and a hundred others without a name; and mountains also, whose names, for the most part, are known only to the Indians. The forest looked like a firm grass sward, and the effect of these lakes in its midst has been well compared, by one who has since visited this same spot, to that of a "mirror broken into a thousand fragments, and wildly scattered over the grass, reflecting the full blaze of the sun."

Setting out on our return to the river, still at an early hour in the day, we decided to follow the course of the torrent, which we supposed to be Murch Brook, as long as it would not lead us too far out of our way. We thus travelled about four miles in the very torrent itself, continually crossing and recrossing it, leaping from rock to rock, and jumping with the stream down falls of seven or eight feet, or sometimes sliding down on our backs in a thin sheet of water. This ravine had been the scene of an extraordinary freshet in the spring, apparently accompanied by a slide from the mountain. It must have been filled with a stream of stones and water, at least twenty feet above the present level of the torrent. For a rod or two, on either side of its channel, the trees were barked and splintered up to their tops, the birches bent over, twisted, and sometimes finely split, like a stable-broom; some, a foot in diameter, snapped off, and whole clumps of trees bent over with the weight of rocks piled on them. In one place we noticed a rock, two or three feet in diameter, lodged nearly twenty feet high in the crotch of a tree. For the whole four miles, we saw but one rill empty-ing in, and the volume of water did not seem to be increased from the first. We travelled thus very rapidly with a downward impetus, and grew remark-ably expert at leaping from rock to rock, for leap we must, and leap we did, whether there was any rock at the right distance or not. It was a pleasant picture when the foremost turned about and looked up the winding ravine, walled in with rocks and the green forest, to see, at intervals of a rod or two, a red-shirted or green-jacketed mountaineer against the white torrent, leaping down the channel with his pack on his back, or pausing upon a convenient rock in the midst of the torrent to mend a rent in his clothes, or unstrap the dipper at his belt to take a draught of the water. At one place we were startled by seeing, on a little sandy shelf by the side of the stream, the fresh print of a man's foot, and for a mo-ment realized how Robinson Crusoe felt in a similar case; but at last we remembered that we had struck this stream on our way up, though we could not have told where, and one had descended into the ravine for a drink.

Perhaps I most fully realized that this was primeval, untamed, and forever untameable *Nature,* or whatever else men call it, while coming down this part of the mountain. We were passing over "Burnt Lands," burnt by lightning, perchance, though they showed no recent marks of fire, hardly so much as a charred stump, but looked rather like a natural pasture for the moose and deer, exceedingly wild and desolate, with occasional strips of timber crossing them, and low poplars springing up, and patches of blueberries here and there. I found myself traversing them familiarly, like some pasture run to waste, or partially reclaimed by man; but when I reflected what man, what brother or sister or kinsman of our race made it and claimed it, I expected the proprietor to rise up and dispute my passage. It is difficult to conceive of a region uninhabited by man. We habitually presume his presence and influence everywhere. And yet we have not seen pure Nature, unless we have seen her thus vast and drear and inhuman, though in the midst of cities. Nature was here something savage and awful, though beautiful. I looked with awe at the ground I trod on, to see what the Powers had made there, the form and fashion and material of their work. This was that Earth of which

we have heard, made out of Chaos and Old Night.
Here was no man's garden, but the unhandselled
globe. It was not lawn, nor pasture, nor mead, nor
woodland, nor lea, nor arable, nor waste-land. It was
the fresh and natural surface of the planet Earth, as
it was made for ever and ever,—to be the dwelling of
man, we say,—so Nature made it, and man may use
it if he can. Man was not to be associated with it. It
was Matter, vast, terrific,—not his Mother Earth
that we have heard of, not for him to tread on, or be
buried in,—no, it were being too familiar even to let
his bones lie there,—the home, this, of Necessity
and Fate. There was there felt the presence of a force
not bound to be kind to man. It was a place for hea-
thenism and superstitious rites,—to be inhabited by
men nearer of kin to the rocks and to wild animals
than we. We walked over it with a certain awe, stop-
ping, from time to time, to pick the blueberries
which grew there, and had a smart and spicy taste.
Perchance where *our* wild pines stand, and leaves lie
on their forest floor, in Concord, there were once
reapers, and husbandmen planted grain; but here
not even the surface had been scarred by man, but it
was a specimen of what God saw fit to make this
world. What is it to be admitted to a museum, to see
a myriad of particular things, compared with being
shown some star's surface, some hard matter in its
home! I stand in awe of my body, this matter to
which I am bound has become so strange to me. I

fear not spirits, ghosts, of which I am one,—*that* my body might,—but I fear bodies, I tremble to meet them. What is this Titan that has possession of me? Talk of mysteries!—Think of our life in nature,— daily to be shown matter, to come in contact with it,—rocks, trees, wind on our cheeks! the *solid* earth! the *actual* world! the *common sense! Contact! Contact! Who* are we? *where* are we?

Erelong we recognized some rocks and other features in the landscape which we had purposely impressed on our memories, and, quickening our pace, by two o'clock we reached the bateau.* Here we had expected to dine on trout, but in this glaring sunlight they were slow to take the bait, so we were compelled to make the most of the crumbs of our hard bread and our pork, which were both nearly exhausted.

About four o'clock, the same afternoon, we commenced our return voyage, which would require but little if any poling. In shooting rapids the boatmen use large and broad paddles, instead of poles, to guide the boat with. Though we glided so swiftly, and often smoothly, down, where it had cost us no slight effort to get up, our present voyage was attended with far more danger: for if we once fairly struck one

---

*The bears had not touched things on our possessions. They sometimes tear a bateau to pieces for the sake of the tar with which it is besmeared.

of the thousand rocks by which we were surrounded
the boat would be swamped in an instant. When
a boat is swamped under these circumstances, the
boatmen commonly find no difficulty in keeping
afloat at first, for the current keeps both them and
their cargo up for a long way down the stream; and if
they can swim, they have only to work their way gradually to the shore. The greatest danger is of being
caught in an eddy behind some larger rock, where
the water rushes up stream faster than elsewhere
it does down, and being carried round and round
under the surface till they are drowned. McCauslin
pointed out some rocks which had been the scene of
a fatal accident of this kind. Sometimes the body is
not thrown out for several hours.

We were soon at the Aboljacarmegus Falls. Anxious to avoid the delay, as well as the labor, of the
portage here, our boatmen went forward first to re-
connoitre, and concluded to let the bateau down the
falls, carrying the baggage only over the portage.
Jumping from rock to rock until nearly in the middle
of the stream, we were ready to receive the boat and
let her down over the first fall, some six or seven feet
perpendicular. The boatmen stand upon the edge of
a shelf of rock, where the fall is perhaps nine or ten
feet perpendicular, in from one to two feet of rapid
water, one on each side of the boat, and let it slide

gently over, till the bow is run out ten or twelve feet in the air; then, letting it drop squarely, while one holds the painter, the other leaps in, and his companion following, they are whirled down the rapids to a new fall, or to smooth water. In a very few minutes they had accomplished a passage in safety, which would be as foolhardy for the unskilful to attempt as the descent of Niagara itself. It seemed as if it needed only a little familiarity, and a little more skill, to navigate down such falls as Niagara itself with safety. At any rate, I should not despair of such men in the rapids above table-rock, until I saw them actually go over the falls, so cool, so collected, so fertile in resources are they. One might have thought that these were falls, and that falls were not to be waded through with impunity, like a mud-puddle. There was really danger of their losing their sublimity in losing their power to harm us. Familiarity breeds contempt. The boatman pauses, perchance, on some shelf beneath a table-rock under the fall, standing in some cove of backwater two feet deep, and you hear his rough voice come up through the spray, coolly giving directions how to launch the boat this time.

Having carried round Pockwockomus Falls, our oars soon brought us to the Katepskonegan, or Oak Hall carry, where we decided to camp half way over, leaving our bateau to be carried over in the morning on fresh shoulders.

* * *

In the morning we carried our boat over and launched it, making haste lest the wind should rise. The boatmen ran down Passamagamet, and, soon after, Ambejijis Falls, while we walked round with the baggage. We made a hasty breakfast at the head of Ambejijis Lake, on the remainder of our pork, and were soon rowing across its smooth surface again, under a pleasant sky, the mountain being now clear of clouds, in the northeast. Taking turns at the oars, we shot rapidly across Deep Cove, the foot of Pamadumcook, and the North Twin, at the rate of six miles an hour, the wind not being high enough to disturb us, and reached the Dam at noon. The boatmen went through one of the log sluices in the bateau, where the fall was ten feet at the bottom, and took us in below. Here was the longest rapid in our voyage, and perhaps the running this was as dangerous and arduous a task as any. Shooting down sometimes at the rate, as we judged, of fifteen miles an hour, if we struck a rock we were split from end to end in an instant. Now, like a bait bobbing from some river monster, amid the eddies, now darting to this side of the stream, now to that, gliding swift and smooth near to our destruction, or striking broad off with the paddle and drawing the boat to right or left with all our might, in order to avoid a rock. I suppose that it was like running the rapids of the Saute de St. Marie, at the outlet of Lake Superior, and our boatmen probably displayed no less dexterity than the Indians there do. We soon ran through this mile, and floated in Quakish Lake.

Thus a man shall lead his life away here on the edge of the wilderness, on Indian Millinocket stream, in a new world, far in the dark of a continent, and have a flute to play at evening here, while his strains echo to the stars, amid the howling of wolves; shall live, as it were, in the primitive age of the world, a primitive man. Yet he shall spend a sunny day, and in this century be my contemporary; perchance shall read some scattered leaves of literature, and sometimes talk with me. Why read history, then, if the ages and the generations are now? He lives three thousand years deep into time, an age not yet described by poets. Can you well go further back in history than this? Ay! ay!—for there turns up but now into the mouth of Millinocket stream a still more ancient and primitive man, whose history is not brought down even to the former. In a bark vessel sewn with the roots of the spruce, with hornbeam paddles, he dips his way along. He is but dim and misty to me, obscured by the aeons that lie between the bark-canoe and the bateau. He builds no house of logs, but a wigwam of skins. He eats no hot bread and sweet cake, but musquash and moose-meat and the fat of bears. He glides up the Millinocket and is lost to my sight, as a more distant and misty cloud is seen flitting by behind a nearer, and is lost in space. So he goes about his destiny, the red face of man.

After having passed the night, and buttered our boots for the last time, at Uncle George's, whose dogs almost devoured him for joy at his return, we kept on down the river the next day, about eight miles on foot, and then took a bateau, with a man to pole it, to Mattawamkeag, ten more. At the middle of that very night, to make a swift conclusion to a long story, we dropped our buggy over the half-finished bridge at Oldtown, where we heard the confused din and clink of a hundred saws, which never rest, and at six o'clock the next morning one of the party was steaming his way to Massachusetts.

The Allegash and East Branch

I STARTED ON my third excursion to the Maine woods Monday, July 20th, 1857, with one companion, arriving at Bangor the next day at noon. We had hardly left the steamer, when we passed Molly Molasses in the street. As long as she lives the Penobscots may be considered extant as a tribe. The succeeding morning, a relative of mine, who is well acquainted with the Penobscot Indians, and who had been my companion in my two previous excursions into the Maine woods, took me in his wagon to Oldtown, to assist me in obtaining an Indian for this expedition. We were ferried across to the Indian Island in a bateau. The ferryman's boy had got the key to it, but the father who was a blacksmith, after a little hesitation, cut the chain with a cold-chisel on a rock. He told us that the Indians were nearly all gone to the seaboard and to Massachusetts, partly on account of the small-pox, of which they are very much afraid, having broken out in Oldtown, and it was doubtful whether we should find a suitable one at home. The old chief Neptune, however, was there still. The first man we saw on the island was an Indian named Joseph Polis, whom my relative had known from a boy, and now addressed familiarly as "Joe." He was dressing a deerskin in his yard. The skin was spread over a slanting log, and he was scraping it with a stick, held by both hands. He was stoutly built, perhaps a little above the middle height, with a broad face, and, as others said, perfect Indian features and complexion. His house was a two-story white one with blinds, the best looking that I noticed there, and as good as an average one on a New England village street. It was surrounded by a garden and fruit-trees, single cornstalks standing thinly amid the beans. We asked him if he knew any good Indian who would like to go into the woods with us, that is, to the Allegash Lakes, by way of Moosehead, and return by the East Branch of the Penobscot, or vary from this as we pleased. To which he answered, out of that strange remoteness in which the Indian ever dwells to the white man, "Me like to go myself; me want to get some moose"; and kept on scraping the skin.

The ferryman had told us that all the best Indians were gone except Polis, who was one of the aristocracy. He to be sure would be the best man we could have, but if he went at all would want a great price; so we did not expect to get him. Polis asked at first two dollars a day, but agreed to go for a dollar and a half, and fifty cents a week for his canoe. He would come to Bangor with his canoe by the seven o'clock train that evening,—we might depend on him. We thought ourselves lucky to secure the services of this man, who was known to be particularly steady and trustworthy.

I spent the afternoon with my companion, who had remained in Bangor, in preparing for our expedition, purchasing provisions, hard bread, pork, coffee, sugar, &c., and some India-rubber clothing.

We had at first thought of exploring the St. John from its source to its mouth, or else to go up the Penobscot by its East Branch to the lakes of the St. John, and return by way of Chesuncook and Moosehead. We had finally inclined to the last route, only reversing the order of it, going by way of Moosehead, and returning by the Penobscot, otherwise it would have been all the way up stream and taken twice as long.

Early the next morning (July 23d) the stage called for us, the Indian having breakfasted with us, and already placed the baggage in the canoe to see how it would go. My companion and I had each a large knapsack as full as it would hold, and we had two large India-rubber bags which held our provision and utensils. As for the Indian, all the baggage he had, beside his axe and gun, was a blanket, which he brought loose in his hand. However, he had laid in a store of tobacco and a new pipe for the excursion.

The canoe was securely lashed diagonally across the top of the stage, with bits of carpet tucked under the edge to prevent its chafing. The very accommodating driver appeared as much accustomed to carrying canoes in this way as bandboxes.

The Indian sat on the front seat, saying nothing to anybody, with a stolid expression of face, as if barely awake to what was going on. Again I was struck by the peculiar vagueness of his replies when addressed in the stage, or at the taverns. He really never said anything on such occasions. He was merely stirred up, like a wild beast, and passively muttered some insignificant response. His answer, in such cases, was never the consequence of a positive mental energy, but vague as a puff of smoke, suggesting no *responsibility,* and if you considered it, you would find that you had got nothing out of him. This was instead of the conventional palaver and smartness of the white man, and equally profitable. Most get no more than this out of the Indian, and pronounce him stolid accordingly. I was surprised to see what a foolish and impertinent style a Maine man, a passenger, used in addressing him, as if he were a child, which only made his eyes glisten a little. A tipsy Canadian asked him at a tavern, in a drawling tone, if he smoked, to which he answered with an indefinite "yes." "Won't you lend me your pipe a little while?" asked the other. He replied, looking straight by the man's head, with a face singularly vacant to all neighboring interests, "Me got no pipe"; yet I had seen him put a new one, with a supply of tobacco, into his pocket that morning.

When we reached the lake, about half past eight in the evening, it was still steadily raining, and harder than before; and, in that fresh, cool atmosphere, the hylodes were peeping and the toads ringing about the lake universally, as in the spring with us. It was as if the seasons had revolved backward two or three months, or I had arrived at the abode of perpetual spring.

We had expected to go upon the lake at once, and after paddling up two or three miles, to camp on one of its islands; but on account of the steady and increasing rain, we decided to go to one of the taverns for the night, though, for my own part, I should have preferred to camp out.

About four o'clock the next morning, (July 24th,) though it was quite cloudy, accompanied by the landlord to the water's edge, in the twilight, we launched our canoe from a rock on the Moosehead Lake.

Paddling along the eastern side of the lake in the still of the morning, we soon saw a few sheldrakes, which the Indian called *Shecorways*, and some peetweets *Naramekechus*, on the rocky shore; we also saw and heard loons, *medawisla*, which he said was a

sign of wind. It was inspiriting to hear the regular dip
of the paddles, as if they were our fins or flippers, and
to realize that we were at length fairly embarked. We
who had felt strangely as stage-passengers and tav-
ern-lodgers were suddenly naturalized there and presented with the freedom of the lakes and the woods.
Having passed the small rocky isles within two or
three miles of the foot of the lake, we had a short
consultation respecting our course, and inclined to
the western shore for the sake of its lee; for otherwise, if the wind should rise, it would be impossible
for us to reach Mount Kineo, which is about midway
up the lake on the east side, but at its narrowest part,
where probably we could recross if we took the western side. The wind is the chief obstacle to crossing
the lakes, especially in so small a canoe.

The Indian said that the usnea lichen which we
saw hanging from the trees was called *chorchorque*.
We asked him the names of several small birds which
we heard this morning. The wood-thrush, which was
quite common, and whose note he imitated, he said
was called *Adelungquamooktum;* but sometimes he
could not tell the name of some small bird which I
heard and knew, but he said, "I tell all the birds about
here,—this country; can't tell littlum noise, but I see
'em, then I can tell."

I observed that I should like to go to school to him
to learn his language, living on the Indian island the

while; could not that be done? "O, yer," he replied, "good many do so." I asked how long he thought it would take. He said one week. I told him that in this voyage I would tell him all I knew, and he should tell me all he knew, to which he readily agreed.

The birds sang quite as in our woods,—the red-eye, red-start, veery, wood-pewee, etc., but we saw no bluebirds in all our journey, and several told me in Bangor that they had not the bluebird there. Mt. Kineo, which was generally visible, though occasionally concealed by islands or the mainland in front, had a level bar of cloud concealing its summit, and all the mountain-tops about the lake were cut off at the same height. Ducks of various kinds—sheldrake, summer ducks, etc.—were quite common, and ran over the water before us as fast as a horse trots. Thus they were soon out of sight.

The Indian asked the meaning of *reality,* as near as I could make out the word, which he said one of us had used; also of *"interrent,"* that is intelligent. I observed that he could rarely sound the letter r, but used l, as also r for l sometimes; as *load* for road, *pickelel* for pickerel, *Soogle* Island for Sugar Island, *lock* for rock, etc. Yet he trilled the r pretty well after me.

I asked him the meaning of the world *Musketicook,* the Indian name of Concord River. He pronounced it *Muskéeticook,* emphasizing the second syllable with a peculiar guttural sound, and said that

it meant "Dead-water," which it is, and in this defi-
nition he agreed exactly with the St. Francis Indian
with whom I talked in 1853.

On a point on the mainland some miles southwest
of Sand-bar Island, where we landed to stretch our
legs and look at the vegetation, going inland a few
steps, I discovered a fire still glowing beneath its
ashes, where somebody had breakfasted, and a bed
of twigs prepared for the following night. So I knew
not only that they had just left, but that they designed to return, and by the breadth of the bed that
there was more than one in the party. You might have
gone within six feet of these signs without seeing
them. There grew the beaked hazel, the only hazel
which I saw on this journey, the *Diervilla,* rue seven
feet high, which was very abundant on all the lake
and river shores, and *Cornus stolonifera,* or red osier,
whose bark, the Indian said, was good to smoke, and
was called *maquoxigill,* "tobacco before white people
came to this country, Indian tobacco."

We approached the land again through pretty
rough water, and then steered directly across the
lake, at its narrowest part, to the eastern side, and
were soon partly under the lee of the mountain,
about a mile north of the Kineo House, having paddled about twenty miles. It was now about noon.

We designed to stop there that afternoon and
night, and spent half an hour looking along the shore

northward for a suitable place to camp. We took out all our baggage at one place in vain, it being too rocky and uneven, and while engaged in this search we made our first acquaintance with the moose-fly. At length, half a mile farther north, by going half a dozen rods into the dense spruce and fir wood on the side of the mountain, almost as dark as a cellar, we found a place sufficiently clear and level to lie down on, after cutting away a few bushes. We required a space only seven feet by six for our bed, the fire being four or five feet in front, though it made no odds how rough the hearth was; but it was not always easy to find this in those woods. The Indian first cleared a path to it from the shore with his axe, and we then carried up all our baggage, pitched our tent, and made our bed, in order to be ready for foul weather, which then threatened us, and for the night. He gathered a large armful of fir twigs, breaking them off, which he said were the best for our bed, partly, I thought, because they were the largest and could be most rapidly collected. It had been raining more or less for four or five days, and the wood was even damper than usual, but he got dry bark for the fire from the under-side of a dead leaning hemlock, which, he said, he could always do.

After dinner we returned southward along the shore, in the canoe, on account of the difficulty of climbing over the rocks and fallen trees, and began

to ascend the mountain along the edge of the precipice. But a smart shower coming up just then, the
Indian crept under his canoe, while we, being protected by our rubber coats, proceeded to botanize.
So we sent him back to the camp for shelter, agree-
ing that he should come there for us with his canoe
toward night. It had rained a little in the forenoon,
and we trusted that this would be the clearing-up
shower, which it proved; but our feet and legs were
thoroughly wet by the bushes. The clouds breaking
away a little, we had a glorious wild view, as we
ascended, of the broad lake with its fluctuating
surface and numerous forest-clad islands, extending
beyond our sight both north and south, and the
boundless forest undulating away from its shores
on every side, as densely packed as a rye-field, and
enveloping nameless mountains in succession; but
above all, looking westward over a large island was
visible a very distant part of the lake, though we did
not then suspect it to be Moosehead,—at first a
mere broken white line seen through the tops of the
island trees, like hay-caps, but spreading to a lake
when we got higher. Beyond this we saw what appears to be called Bald Mountain on the map, some
twenty-five miles distant, near the sources of the
Penobscot. It was a perfect lake of the woods. But
this was only a transient gleam, for the rain was not
quite over.

Looking southward, the heavens were completely

overcast, the mountains capped with clouds, and the lake generally wore a dark and stormy appearance, but from its surface just north of Sugar Island, six or eight miles distant, there was reflected upward to us through the misty air a bright blue tinge from the distant unseen sky of another latitude beyond. They probably had a clear sky then at Greenville, the south end of the lake. Standing on a mountain in the midst of a lake, where would you look for the first sign of approaching fair weather? Not into the heavens, it seems, but into the lake.

On reaching the canoe we found that [the Indian] had caught a lake trout weighing about three pounds, at the depth of twenty-five or thirty feet, while we were on the mountain.

When we got to the camp, the canoe was taken out and turned over, and a log laid across it to prevent its being blown away. The Indian cut some large logs of damp and rotten hard wood to smoulder and keep fire through the night. The trout was fried for supper. Our tent was of thin cotton cloth and quite small, forming with the ground a triangular prism closed at the rear end, six feet long, seven wide, and four high, so that we could barely sit up in the middle. It required two forked stakes, a smooth ridge-pole, and a dozen or more pins to pitch it. It kept off dew and wind, and an ordinary rain, and answered our purpose well enough. We reclined within it till bedtime, each with his baggage at his head, or else sat about the fire, having hung our wet clothes on a pole before the fire for the night.

It was a dense and damp spruce and fir wood in which we lay, and, except for our fire, perfectly dark; and when I awoke in the night, I either heard an owl from deeper in the forest behind us, or a loon from a distance over the lake. Getting up some time after midnight to collect the scattered brands together, while my companions were sound asleep, I observed, partly in the fire, which had ceased to blaze, a perfectly regular elliptical ring of light, about five inches in its shortest diameter, six or seven in its longer, and from one eighth to one quarter of an inch wide. It was fully as bright as the fire, but not reddish or scarlet like a coal, but a white and slumbering light, like the glowworm's. I could tell it from the fire only by its whiteness. I saw at once that it must be phosphorescent wood, which I had so often heard of, but never chanced to see. Putting my finger on it, with a little hesitation, I found that it was a piece of dead moosewood (*Acer striatum*) which the Indian had cut off in a slanting direction the evening before. Using my knife, I discovered that the light proceeded from that portion of the sap-wood immediately under the bark, and thus presented a regular ring at the end, which, indeed, appeared raised above the level of the wood, and when I pared off the bark and cut into the sap, it was all aglow along the log. I was surprised to find the wood quite hard and apparently sound, though probably decay had commenced in the sap, and I cut out some little triangular chips, and placing them in the hollow of my hand, carried them into the camp, waked my companion, and showed them to him. They lit up the inside of my hand, revealing the lines and wrinkles, and appearing exactly like coals of fire raised to a white heat, and I saw at once how, probably, the Indian jugglers had imposed on their people and on travellers, pretending to hold coals of fire in their mouths.

I also noticed that part of a decayed stump within four or five feet of the fire, an inch wide and six inches long, soft and shaking wood, shone with equal brightness.

I neglected to ascertain whether our fire had anything to do with this, but the previous day's rain and long-continued wet weather undoubtedly had.

I was exceedingly interested by this phenomenon, and already felt paid for my journey. It could hardly have thrilled me more if it had taken the form of letters, or of the human face. If I had met with this ring of light while groping in this forest alone, away from any fire, I should have been still more surprised. I little thought that there was such a light shining in the darkness of the wilderness for me.

The next day the Indian told me their name for this light,—*Artoosoqu'*,—and on my inquiring con-

cerning the will-o'-the-wisp, and the like phenomena, he said that his "folks" sometimes saw fires passing along at various heights, even as high as the trees,
and making a noise. I was prepared after this to hear
of the most startling and unimagined phenomena
witnessed by "his folks," they are abroad at all hours
and seasons in scenes so unfrequented by white
men. Nature must have made a thousand revelations
to them which are still secrets to us.

I did not regret my not having seen this before,
since I now saw it under circumstances so favorable.
I was in just the frame of mind to see something
wonderful, and this was a phenomenon adequate to
my circumstances and expectation, and it put me on
the alert to see more like it. I exulted like "a pagan
suckled in a creed" that had never been worn at all,
but was bran new, and adequate to the occasion. I let
science slide, and rejoiced in that light as if it had
been a fellow-creature. I saw that it was excellent,
and was very glad to know that it was so cheap. A sci-
entific *explanation,* as it is called, would have been
altogether out of place there. That is for pale daylight. Science with its retorts would have put me to
sleep; it was the opportunity to be ignorant that I improved. It suggested to me that there was something
to be seen if one had eyes. It made a believer of me
more than before. I believed that the woods were not
tenantless, but choke-full of honest spirits as good
as myself any day,—not an empty chamber, in which

chemistry was left to work alone, but an inhabited house,—and for a few moments I enjoyed fellowship with them. Your so-called wise man goes trying to persuade himself that there is no entity there but himself and his traps, but it is a great deal easier to believe the truth. It suggested, too, that the same experience always gives birth to the same sort of belief or religion. One revelation has been made to the Indian, another to the white man. I have much to learn of the Indian, nothing of the missionary. I am not sure but all that would tempt me to teach the Indian my religion would be his promise to teach me *his*. Long enough I had heard of irrelevant things; now at length I was glad to make acquaintance with the light that dwells in rotten wood. Where is all your knowledge gone to? It evaporates completely, for it has no depth.

We crossed a deep and wide bay which makes eastward north of Kineo, leaving an island on our left, and keeping up the eastern side of the lake. This way or that led to some Tomhegan or *Socatarian* stream, up which the Indian had hunted, and whither I longed to go. The last name, however, had a bogus sound, too much like sectarian for me, as if a missionary had tampered with it; but I know that the Indians were very liberal. I think I should have inclined to the Tomhegan first.

We then crossed another broad bay, which, as we

could no longer observe the shore particularly, afforded ample time for conversation. The Indian said
that he had got his money by hunting, mostly high up
the west branch of the Penobscot, and toward the
head of the St. John; he had hunted there from a boy,
and knew all about that region. His game had been,
beaver, otter, black cat (or fisher), sable, moose, &c.
Loup cervier (or Canada lynx) were plenty yet in
burnt grounds. For food in the woods, he uses partridges, ducks, dried moose-meat, hedge-hog, &c.
Loons, too, were good, only "bile 'em good." He told
us at some length how he had suffered from starvation when a mere lad, being overtaken by winter
when hunting with two grown Indians in the northern part of Maine, and obliged to leave their canoe
on account of ice.

Pointing into the bay, he said that it was the way to
various lakes which he knew. Only solemn bear-
haunted mountains, with their great wooded slopes,
were visible; where, as man is not, we suppose some
other power to be. My imagination personified the
slopes themselves, as if by their very length they
would waylay you, and compel you to camp again on
them before night. Some invisible glutton would
seem to drop from the trees and gnaw at the heart of
the solitary hunter who threaded those woods; and
yet I was tempted to walk there. The Indian said that
he had been along there several times.

I asked him how he guided himself in the woods.

"O," said he, "I can tell good many ways." When I pressed him further, he answered, "Sometimes I lookum side-hill," and he glanced toward a high hill or mountain on the eastern shore, "great difference between the north and south, see where the sun has shone most. So trees,—the large limbs bend toward south. Sometimes I lookum locks" (rocks). I asked what he saw on the rocks, but he did not describe anything in particular, answering vaguely, in a mysterious or drawling tone, "Bare locks on lake shore,—great difference between N. S. E. W. side,—can tell what the sun has shone on." "Suppose," said I, "that I should take you in a dark night, right up here into the middle of the woods a hundred miles, set you down, and turn you round quickly twenty times, could you steer straight to Oldtown?" "O yer," said he, "have done pretty much same thing. I will tell you. Some years ago I met an old white hunter at Millinocket; very good hunter. He said he could go anywhere in the woods. He wanted to hunt with me that day, so we start. We chase a moose all the forenoon, round and round, till middle of afternoon, when we kill him. Then I said to him, now you go straight to camp. Don't go round and round where we've been, but go straight. He said, I can't do that, I don't know where I am. Where you think camp? I asked. He pointed so. Then I laugh at him. I take the lead and go right off the other way, cross our tracks many times, straight camp." "How do you do that?"

asked I. "O, I can't tell *you*," he replied. "Great difference between me and white man."

It appeared as if the sources of information were so various that he did not give a distinct, conscious attention to any one, and so could not readily refer to any when questioned about it, but he found his way very much as an animal does. Perhaps what is commonly called instinct in the animal, in this case is merely a sharpened and educated sense. Often, when an Indian says, "I don't know," in regard to the route he is to take, he does not mean what a white man would by those words, for his Indian instinct may tell him still as much as the most confident white man knows. He does not carry things in his head, nor remember the route exactly, like a white man, but relies on himself at the moment. Not having experienced the need of the other sort of knowledge, all labelled and arranged, he has not acquired it.

Sunday, July 26

The note of the white-throated sparrow, a very inspiriting but almost wiry sound, was the first heard in the morning, and with this all the woods rang. This was the prevailing bird in the northern part of Maine. The forest generally was all alive with them at this season, and they were proportionally numerous and musical about Bangor. They evidently breed in that State. Wilson did not know where they bred, and says, "Their only note is a kind of chip." Though commonly unseen, their simple *ah, te-te-te, te-te-te, te-te-te,* so sharp and piercing, was as distinct to the ear as the passage of a spark of fire shot into the darkest of the forest would be to the eye. I thought that they commonly uttered it as they flew. I hear this note for a few days only in the spring, as they go through Concord, and in the fall see them again going southward, but then they are mute. We were commonly aroused by their lively strain very early. What a glorious time they must have in that wilderness, far from mankind and election day!

We carried a part of the baggage about Pine Stream Falls, while the Indian went down in the canoe. A Bangor merchant had told us that two men in his employ were drowned some time ago while passing these falls in a bateau, and a third clung to a rock all night, and was taken off in the morning. There were magnificent great purple-fringed orchises on this carry and the neighboring shores. I measured the largest canoe-birch which I saw in this journey near the end of the carry. It was 14$^{1}/_{2}$ feet in circumference at two feet from the ground, but at five feet divided into three parts. The canoe-birches thereabouts were commonly marked by conspicuous dark spiral ridges, with a groove between, so that I thought at first that they had been struck by lightning, but, as the Indian said, it was evidently caused by the grain of the tree. He cut a small, woody knob, as big as a filbert, from the trunk of a fir, apparently an old balsam vesicle filled with wood, which he said was good medicine.

After we had embarked and gone half a mile, my companion remembered that he had left his knife, and we paddled back to get it, against the strong and swift current. This taught us the difference between going up and down the stream, for while we were working our way back a quarter of a mile, we should have gone down a mile and a half at least. So we landed, and while he and the Indian were gone back for it, I watched the motions of the foam, a kind of white water-fowl near the shore, forty or fifty rods below. It alternately appeared and disappeared behind the rock, being carried round by an eddy. Even this semblance of life was interesting on that lonely river.

Immediately below these falls was the Chesuncook dead-water, caused by the flowing back of the lake. As we paddled slowly over this, the Indian told us a story of his hunting thereabouts, and something more interesting about himself. It appeared that he had represented his tribe at Augusta, and also once at Washington, where he had met some Western chiefs. He had been consulted at Augusta, and gave advice, which he said was followed, respecting the eastern boundary of Maine, as determined by highlands and streams, at the time of the difficulties on

that side. He was employed with the surveyors on
the line. Also he had called on Daniel Webster in
Boston, at the time of his Bunker Hill oration.

I was surprised to hear him say that he liked to go
to Boston, New York, Philadelphia, &c., &c.; that he
would like to live there. But then, as if relenting a little, when he thought what a poor figure he would
make there, he added, "I suppose, I live in New York,
I be poorest hunter, I expect." He understood very
well both his superiority and his inferiority to the
whites. He criticised the people of the United States
as compared with other nations, but the only distinct
idea with which he labored was, that they were "very
strong," but, like some individuals, "too fast."

About noon we turned northward, up a broad
kind of estuary, and at its northeast corner found the
Caucomgomoc River, and after going about a mile
from the lake, reached the Umbazookskus, which
comes in on the right at a point where the former river, coming from the west, turns short to the
south. Our course was up the Umbazookskus, but
as the Indian knew of a good camping-place, that is,
a cool place where there were few mosquitoes,
about half a mile farther up the Caucomgomoc, we
went thither. The latter river, judging from the map,
is the longer and principal stream, and, therefore, its
name must prevail below the junction. So quickly
we changed the civilizing sky of Chesuncook for the

dark wood of the Caucomgomoc. On reaching the Indian's camping-ground, on the south side, where the bank was about a dozen feet high, I read on the trunk of a fir-tree blazed by an axe an inscription in charcoal which had been left by him. It was surmounted by a drawing of a bear paddling a canoe, which he said was the sign which had been used by his family always. The drawing, though rude, could not be mistaken for anything but a bear, and he doubted my ability to copy it. The inscription ran thus, *verbatim et literatim.* I interline the English of his Indian as he gave it to me.

July 26,
1853.

Niasoseb
We alone Joseph
Polis elioi
Polis start
sia olta
for Oldtown
onke ni
right away.
quambi

July 15,
1855.
Niasoseb.

He added now below:—

1857,
July 26.
Io.   Polis.

This was one of his homes. I saw where he had sometimes stretched his moose-hides on the opposite or sunny north side of the river, where there was a narrow meadow.

The Indian said that the Umbazookskus, being a dead stream with broad meadows, was a good place for moose, and he frequently came a-hunting here, being out alone three weeks or more from Oldtown. He sometimes, also, went a-hunting to the Seboois Lakes, taking the stage, with his gun and ammunition, axe and blankets, hard bread and pork, perhaps for a hundred miles of the way, and jumped off at the wildest place on the road, where he was at once at home, and every rod was a tavern-site for him. Then, after a short journey through the woods, he would build a spruce-bark canoe in one day, putting but few ribs into it, that it might be light, and after doing his hunting with it on the lakes, would return with his furs the same way he had come. Thus you have an Indian availing himself cunningly of the advantages of civilization, without losing any of his woodcraft, but proving himself the more successful hunter for it.

This man was very clever and quick to learn anything in his line. Our tent was of a kind new to him; but when he had once seen it pitched it was surprising how quickly he would find and prepare the pole and forked stakes to pitch it with, cutting and placing them right the first time, though I am sure that the majority of white men would have blundered several times.

Monday, July 27

Having rapidly loaded the canoe, which the Indian always carefully attended to, that it might be well trimmed, and each having taken a look, as usual, to see that nothing was left, we set out again, descending the Caucomgomoc, and turning northeasterly up the *Umbazookskus*. This name, the Indian said, meant *Much Meadow River*. We found it a very meadowy stream, and dead water, and now very wide on account of the rains, though, he said, it was sometimes quite narrow. The space between the woods, chiefly bare meadow, was from fifty to two hundred rods in breadth, and is a rare place for moose. It reminded me of the Concord; and what increased the resemblance, was one old musquash house almost afloat.

In the water on the meadows grew sedges, wool-grass, the common blue-flag abundantly, its flower just showing itself above the high water, as if it were a blue water-lily, and higher in the meadows a great many clumps of a peculiar narrow-leaved willow (*Salix petiolaris*), which is common in our river meadows. It was the prevailing one here, and the Indian said that the musquash ate much of it; and here also grew the red osier (*Cornus stolonifera*), its large fruit now whitish.

Though it was still early in the morning, we saw night-hawks circling over the meadow, and as usual heard the *Pepe (Muscicapa Cooperi)*, which is one of the prevailing birds in these woods, and the robin.

It was unusual for the woods to be so distant from the shore, and there was quite an echo from them, but when I was shouting in order to awake it, the Indian reminded me that I should scare the moose, which he was looking out for, and which we all wanted to see. The word for echo was *Pockadunk-quaywayle*.

A broad belt of dead larch-trees along the distant edge of the meadow, against the forest on each side, increased the usual wildness of the scenery. The Indian called these juniper, and said that they had been killed by the back water caused by the dam at the outlet of Chesuncook Lake, some twenty miles distant. I plucked at the water's edge the *Asclepias incarnata,* with quite handsome flowers, a brighter red

than our variety (the *pulchra*). It was the only form of
it which I saw there.

Having paddled several miles up the Umbazookskus, it suddenly contracted to a mere brook, narrow
and swift, the larches and other trees approaching
the bank and leaving no open meadow, and we
landed to get a black-spruce pole for pushing against
the stream. This was the first occasion for one. The
one selected was quite slender, cut about ten feet
long, merely whittled to a point, and the bark shaved
off. The stream, though narrow and swift, was still
deep, with a muddy bottom, as I proved by diving
to it. Beside the plants which I have mentioned, I
observed on the bank here the *Salix cordata* and
rostrata, Ranunculus recurvatus, and *Rubus triflorus*
with ripe fruit.

While we were thus employed, two Indians in a
canoe hove in sight round the bushes, coming down
stream. Our Indian knew one of them, an old man,
and fell into conversation with him in Indian. He belonged at the foot of Moosehead. The other was of
another tribe. They were returning from hunting. I
asked the younger if they had seen any moose, to
which he said no; but I, seeing the moose-hides
sticking out from a great bundle made with their
blankets in the middle of the canoe, added, "Only
their hides." As he was a foreigner, he may have
wished to deceive me, for it is against the law for
white men and foreigners to kill moose in Maine at

this season. But, perhaps, he need not have been alarmed, for the moose-wardens are not very particular. I heard quite directly of one, who being asked by a white man going into the woods what he would say if he killed a moose, answered, "If you bring me a quarter of it, I guess you won't be troubled." His duty being, as he said, only to prevent the "indiscriminate" slaughter of them for their hides. I suppose that he would consider it an *indiscriminate* slaughter when a quarter was not reserved for himself. Such are the perquisites of this office.

Umbazookskus Lake is the head of the Penobscot in this direction, and Mud Pond is the nearest head of the Allegash, one of the chief sources of the St. John. Hodge, who went through this way to the St. Lawrence in the service of the State, calls the portage here a mile and three quarters long, and states that Mud Pond has been found to be fourteen feet higher than Umbazookskus Lake. As the west branch of the Penobscot at the Moosehead carry is considered about twenty-five feet lower than Moosehead Lake, it appears that the Penobscot in the upper part of its course runs in a broad and shallow valley, between the Kennebec and St. Johns, and lower than either of them, though, judging from the map, you might expect it to be the highest.

Mud Pond is about half-way from Umbazookskus to Chamberlain Lake, into which it empties, and to

which we were bound. The Indian said that this was
the wettest carry in the State, and as the season was
a very wet one, we anticipated an unpleasant walk.
As usual he made one large bundle of the pork-keg,
cooking utensils, and other loose traps, by tying them
up in his blanket. We should be obliged to go over
the carry twice, and our method was to carry one half
part way, and then go back for the rest.

The Indian with his canoe soon disappeared before us; but erelong he came back and told us to
take a path which turned off westward, it being better walking, and, at my suggestion, he agreed to
leave a bough in the regular carry at that place, that
we might not pass it by mistake. Thereafter, he said,
we were to keep the main path, and he added, "You
see 'em my tracks." But I had not much faith that
we could distinguish his tracks, since others had
passed over the carry within a few days.
We turned off at the right place, but were soon
confused by numerous logging-paths, coming into
the one we were on, by which lumberers had been to
pick out those pines which I have mentioned. However, we kept what we considered the main path,
though it was a winding one, and in this, at long intervals, we distinguished a faint trace of a footstep.
This, though comparatively unworn, was at first a
better, or, at least, a drier road, than the regular carry
which we had left. It led through an arbor-vitae

wilderness of the grimmest character. The great fallen and rotting trees had been cut through and rolled aside, and their huge trunks abutted on the path on each side, while others still lay across it two or three feet high. It was impossible for us to discern the Indian's trail in the elastic moss, which, like a thick carpet, covered every rock and fallen tree, as well as the earth. Nevertheless, I did occasionally detect the track of a man, and I gave myself some credit for it. I carried my whole load at once, a heavy knapsack, and a large India-rubber bag, containing our bread and a blanket, swung on a paddle; in all, about sixty pounds; but my companion preferred to make two journeys, by short stages, while I waited for him. We could not be sure that we were not depositing our loads each time farther off from the true path.

As I sat waiting for my companion, he would seem to be gone a long time, and I had ample opportunity to make observations on the forest. I now first began to be seriously molested by the black-fly, a very small but perfectly formed fly of that color, about one tenth of an inch long, which I first felt, and then saw, in swarms about me, as I sat by a wider and more than usually doubtful fork in this dark forest-path. The hunters tell bloody stories about them,—how they settle in a ring about your neck, before you know it, and are wiped off in great numbers with your blood. But remembering that I had a wash in my knapsack, prepared by a thoughtful hand in Bangor, I made

haste to apply it to my face and hands, and was glad
to find it effectual, as long as it was fresh, or for
twenty minutes, not only against black-flies, but all
the insects that molested us. They would not alight
on the part thus defended. It was composed of sweet-
oil and oil of turpentine, with a little oil of spearmint,
and camphor. However, I finally concluded that the
remedy was worse than the disease. It was so dis-
agreeable and inconvenient to have your face and
hands covered with such a mixture.

Three large slate-colored birds of the jay genus
(*Garrulus Canadensis*), the Canada-jay, moose-bird,
meat-bird, or what not, came flitting silently and by
degrees toward me, and hopped down the limbs in-
quisitively to within seven or eight feet. They were
more clumsy and not nearly so handsome as the
blue-jay. Fish-hawks, from the lake, uttered their
sharp whistling notes low over the top of the forest
near me, as if they were anxious about a nest there.

After I had sat there some time, I noticed at this
fork in the path a tree which had been blazed, and
the letters "Chamb. L." written on it with red chalk.
This I knew to mean Chamberlain Lake. So I concluded that on the whole we were on the right
course, though as we had come nearly two miles, and
saw no signs of Mud Pond, I did harbor the suspicion
that we might be on a direct course to Chamberlain
Lake, leaving out Mud Pond. This I found by my

map would be about five miles northeasterly, and I then took the bearing by my compass.

My companion having returned with his bag, and also defended his face and hands with the insect-wash, we set forward again. The walking rapidly grew worse, and the path more indistinct, and at length, after passing through a patch of *calla palustris,* still abundantly in bloom, we found ourselves in a more open and regular swamp, made less passable than ordinary by the unusual wetness of the season. We sank a foot deep in water and mud at every step, and sometimes up to our knees, and the trail was almost obliterated, being no more than that a musquash leaves in similar places, when he parts the floating sedge. In fact, it probably was a musquash trail in some places. We concluded that if Mud Pond was as muddy as the approach to it was wet, it certainly deserved its name. It would have been amusing to behold the dogged and deliberate pace at which we entered that swamp, without interchanging a word, as if determined to go through it, though it should come up to our necks. Having penetrated a considerable distance into this, and found a tussuck on which we could deposit our loads, though there was no place to sit, my companion went back for the rest of his pack.

After a long while my companion came back, and the Indian with him. We had taken the wrong road, and the Indian had lost us. He had very wisely gone back to the Canadian's camp, and asked him which way we had probably gone, since he could better understand the ways of white men, and he told him correctly that we had undoubtedly taken the supply road to Chamberlain Lake (slender supplies they would get over such a road at this season). The Indian was greatly surprised that we should have taken what he called a "tow" (i.e. tote or toting or supply) road, instead of a carry path,—that we had not followed his tracks,—said it was "strange," and evidently thought little of our woodcraft.

Having held a consultation, and eaten a mouthful of bread we concluded that it would, perhaps, be nearer for us two now to keep on to Chamberlain Lake, omitting Mud Pond, than to go back and start anew for the last place, though the Indian had never been through this way, and knew nothing about it. In the meanwhile he would go back and finish carrying over his canoe and bundle to Mud Pond, cross that, and go down its outlet and up Chamberlain Lake, and trust to meet us there before night. It was now a little after noon. He supposed that the water in which we stood had flowed back from Mud Pond, which could not be far off eastward, but was unapproachable through the dense cedar swamp.

Making a logging-road in the Maine woods is called "swamping it," and they who do the work are called "swampers." I now perceived the fitness of the term. This was the most perfectly swamped of all the roads I ever saw. Nature must have co-operated with art here. However, I suppose they would tell you that this name took its origin from the fact that the chief work of road-makers in those woods is to make the swamps passable. We came to a stream where the bridge, which had been made of logs tied together with cedar bark, had been broken up, and we got over as we could. This probably emptied into Mud Pond, and perhaps the Indian might have come up it and taken us in there if he had known it. Such as it was, this ruined bridge was the chief evidence that we were on a path of any kind.

We then crossed another low rising ground, and I, who wore shoes, had an opportunity to wring out my stockings, but my companion, who used boots, had found that this was not a safe experiment for him, for he might not be able to get his wet boots on again. He went over the whole ground, or water, three times, for which reason our progress was very slow; beside that the water softened our feet, and to some extent unfitted them for walking. As I sat waiting for him, it would naturally seem an unaccountable time that he was gone. Therefore, as I could see through the woods that the sun was getting low, and it was uncertain how far the lake might be, even if we were on the right course, and in what part of the world we should find ourselves at nightfall, I proposed that I should push through with what speed I could, leaving boughs to mark my path, and find the lake and the Indian, if possible, before night, and send the latter back to carry my companion's bag.

Having gone about a mile, and got into low ground again, I heard a noise like the note of an owl, which I soon discovered to be made by the Indian, and answering him, we soon came together. He had reached the lake, after crossing Mud Pond, and running some rapids below it, and had come up about a mile and a half on our path. If he had not come back to meet us, we probably should not have found him that night, for the path branched once or twice before reaching this particular part of the lake. So he went back for my companion and his bag, while I kept on. Having waded through another stream where the bridge of logs had been broken up and half floated away,—and this was not altogether worse than our ordinary walking, since it was less muddy,— we continued on, through alternate mud and water, to the shore of Apmoojenegamook Lake, which we reached in season for a late supper, instead of dining there, as we had expected, having gone without our dinner. It was at least five miles by the way we had come, and as my companion had gone over most of it three times, he had walked full a dozen miles, bad as it was. In the winter, when the water is frozen, and the snow is four feet deep, it is no doubt a tolerable path to a footman. As it was, I would not have missed that walk for a good deal. If you want an exact recipe for making such a road, take one part Mud Pond, and dilute it with equal parts of Umbazook-skus and Apmoojenegamook; then send a family of musquash through to locate it, look after the grades and culverts, and finish it to their minds, and let a hurricane follow to do the fencing.

We had come out on a point extending into Ap-moojenegamook, or Chamberlain Lake, west of the outlet of Mud Pond, where there was a broad, grav-elly, and rocky shore, encumbered with bleached logs and trees. We were rejoiced to see such dry things in that part of the world. But at first we did not attend to dryness so much as to mud and wetness. We all three walked into the lake up to our middle to wash our clothes.

A belt of dead trees stood all around the lake, some far out in the water, with others prostrate be-hind them, and they made the shore, for the most part, almost inaccessible. This is the effect of the dam at the outlet. Thus the natural sandy or rocky shore, with its green fringe, was concealed and de-stroyed. We coasted westward along the north side, searching for the outlet, about one quarter of a mile distant from this savage-looking shore, on which the waves were breaking violently, knowing that it might easily be concealed amid this rubbish, or by the over-lapping of the shore. It is remarkable how little these important gates to a lake are blazoned. There is no triumphal arch over the modest inlet or outlet, but at some undistinguished point it trickles in or out through the uninterrupted forest, almost as through a sponge.

We reached the outlet in about an hour, and carried over the dam there, which is quite a solid structure, and about one quarter of a mile farther there was a second dam. The reader will perceive that the result of this particular damming about Chamberlain Lake is, that the head-waters of the St. John are made to flow by Bangor. They have thus dammed all the larger lakes, raising their broad surfaces many feet; Moose-head, for instance, some forty miles long, with its steamer on it; thus turning the forces of nature against herself, that they might float their spoils out of the country. They rapidly run out of these immense forests all the finer, and more accessible pine timber, and then leave the bears to watch the decaying dams, not clearing nor cultivating the land, nor making roads, nor building houses, but leaving it a wilderness, as they found it. In many parts, only these dams remain, like deserted beaver-dams. Think how much land they have flowed, without asking Nature's leave! When the State wishes to endow an academy or university, it grants it a tract of forest land: one saw represents an academy; a gang, a university.

The wilderness experiences a sudden rise of all

her streams and lakes, she feels ten thousand vermin gnawing at the base of her noblest trees, many combining, drag them off, jarring over the roots of the survivors, and tumble them into the nearest stream, till the fairest having fallen, they scamper off to ransack some new wilderness, and all is still again. It is as when a migrating army of mice girdles a forest of pines. The chopper fells trees from the same motive that the mouse gnaws them,—to get his living. You tell me that he has a more interesting family than the mouse. That is as it happens. He speaks of a "berth" of timber, a good place for him to get into, just as a worm might. When the chopper would praise a pine, he will commonly tell you that the one he cut was so big that a yoke of oxen stood on its stump; as if that were what the pine had grown for, to become the footstool of oxen. In my mind's eye, I can see these unwieldy tame deer, with a yoke binding them together, and brazen-tipped horns betraying their servitude, taking their stand on the stump of each giant pine in succession throughout this whole forest, and chewing their cud there, until it is nothing but an oxpasture, and run out at that. As if it were good for the oxen, and some terebinthine or other medicinal quality ascended into their nostrils. Or is their elevated position intended merely as a symbol of the fact that the pastoral comes next in order to the sylvan or hunter life?

The character of the logger's admiration is be-
trayed by his very mode of expressing it. If he told all
that was in his mind, he would say, it was so big that
I cut it down and then a yoke of oxen could stand on
its stump. He admires the log, the carcass or corpse,
more than the tree. Why, my dear sir, the tree might
have stood on its own stump, and a great deal more
comfortably and firmly than a yoke of oxen can, if
you had not cut it down. What right have you to cel-
ebrate the virtues of the man you murdered?

The Anglo-American can indeed cut down, and
grub up all this waving forest, and make a stump
speech, and vote for Buchanan on its ruins, but he
cannot converse with the spirit of the tree he fells, he
cannot read the poetry and mythology which retire
as he advances. He ignorantly erases mythological
tablets in order to print his handbills and town-meet-
ing warrants on them. Before he has learned his a b c
in the beautiful but mystic lore of the wilderness
which Spenser and Dante had just begun to read, he
cuts it down, coins a *pine-tree* shilling, (as if to signify
the pine's value to him,) puts up a *dee*strict school-
house, and introduces Webster's spelling-book.

Rounding a point, we stood across a bay for a mile
and a half or two miles, toward a large island, three or
four miles down the lake. We met with ephemeræ
(shad-fly) midway, about a mile from the shore, and
they evidently fly over the whole lake. On Moose-

head I had seen a large devil's-needle half a mile from the shore, coming from the middle of the lake, where it was three or four miles wide at least. It had probably crossed. But at last, of course, you come to lakes so large that an insect cannot fly across them; and this, perhaps, will serve to distinguish a large lake from a small one.

We landed on the southeast side of the island, which was rather elevated, and densely wooded, with a rocky shore, in season for an early dinner. Somebody had camped there not long before, and left the frame on which they stretched a moose-hide, which our Indian criticised severely, thinking it showed but little woodcraft. Here were plenty of the shells of crayfish, or fresh-water lobsters, which had been washed ashore, such as have given a name to some ponds and streams. They are commonly four or five inches long. The Indian proceeded at once to cut a canoe-birch, slanted it up against another tree on the shore, tying it with a withe, and lay down to sleep in its shade.

We had now seen the largest of the Allegash Lakes. The next dam "was about fifteen miles" farther north, down the Allegash, and it was dead water so far. We had been told in Bangor of a man who lived alone, a sort of hermit, at that dam, to take care of it, who spent his time tossing a bullet from one hand to the other, for want of employment,—as if we might want to call on him. This sort of tit-for-tat intercourse between his two hands, bandying to and fro a leaden subject, seems to have been his symbol for society.

This island, according to the map, was about a hundred and ten miles in a straight line north-north-west from Bangor, and about ninety-nine miles east-southeast from Quebec. There was another island visible toward the north end of the lake, with an elevated clearing on it; but we learned afterward that it was not inhabited, had only been used as a pasture for cattle which summered in these woods, though our informant said that there was a hut on the mainland near the outlet of the lake. This unnaturally smooth-shaven, squarish spot, in the midst of the otherwise uninterrupted forest, only reminded us how uninhabited the country was. You would sooner expect to meet with a bear than an ox in such a clearing. At any rate, it must have been a surprise to the bears when they came across it. Such, seen far or near, you know at once to be man's work, for Nature never does it. In order to let in the light to the earth as on a lake, he clears off the forest on the hillsides and plains, and sprinkles fine grass-seed, like an enchanter, and so carpets the earth with a firm sward.

In the mean while, the wind, increasing, blew down the Indian's birch and created such a sea that we found ourselves prisoners on the island, the nearest shore, which was the western, being perhaps a mile distant, and we took the canoe out to prevent its drifting away. We did not know but we should be compelled to spend the rest of the day and the night there. At any rate, the Indian went to sleep again in the shade of his birch, my companion busied himself drying his plants, and I rambled along the shore westward, which was quite stony, and obstructed with fallen bleached or drifted trees for four or five rods in width. I found growing on this broad rocky and gravelly shore the *Salix rostrata, discolor,* and *lucida, Ranunculus recurvatus, Potentilla Norvegica, Scutellaria lateriflora, Eupatorium purpureum, Aster Tradescanti, Mentha Canadensis, Epilobium angustifolium,* abundant, *Lycopus sinuatus, Solidago lanceolata, Spirea salicifolia, Antennaria margaritacea, Prunella, Rumex acetosella,* Raspberries, Wool-grass, *Onoclea,* &c. The nearest trees were *Betula papyracea* and *excelsa,* and *Populus tremuloides.* I give these names because it was my farthest northern point.

Our Indian said that he was a doctor, and could tell me some medicinal use for every plant I could show him. I immediately tried him. He said that the inner bark of the aspen (*Populus tremuloides*) was good for sore eyes; and so with various other plants, proving himself as good as his word. According to his account, he had acquired such knowledge in his youth from a wise old Indian with whom he associated, and he lamented that the present generation of Indians "had lost a great deal."

An Indian at Oldtown had told us that we should be obliged to carry ten miles between Telos Lake on the St. John's and Second Lake on the East Branch of the Penobscot; but the lumberers whom we met assured us that there would not be more than a mile of carry. It turned out that the Indian, who had lately been over this route, was nearest right, as far as we were concerned. However, if one of us could have assisted the Indian in managing the canoe in the rapids, we might have run the greater part of the way; but as he was alone in the management of the canoe in such places, we were obliged to walk the greater part. I did not feel quite ready to try such an experiment on Webster Stream, which has so bad a reputation. According to my observation, a bateau, properly manned, shoots rapids as a matter of course, which a single Indian with a canoe carries round.

My companion and I carried a good part of the baggage on our shoulders, while the Indian took that which would be least injured by wet in the canoe. We did not know when we should see him again, for he had not been this way since the canal was cut, not for more than thirty years. He agreed to stop when he got to smooth water, come up and find our path if he could, and halloo for us, and after waiting a reasonable time go on and try again,—and we were to look out in like manner for him.

He commenced by running through the sluice-way and over the dam, as usual, standing up in his tossing canoe, and was soon out of sight behind a point in a wild gorge. This Webster Stream is well known to lumbermen as a difficult one. It is exceedingly rapid and rocky, and also shallow, and can hardly be considered navigable, unless that may mean that what is launched in it is sure to be carried swiftly down it, though it may be dashed to pieces by the way. It is somewhat like navigating a thunderspout. With commonly an irresistible force urging you on, you have got to choose your own course each moment, between the rocks and shallows, and to get into it, moving forward always with the utmost possible moderation, and often holding on, if you can, that you may inspect the rapids before you.

By the Indian's direction we took an old path on the south side, which appeared to keep down the stream, though at a considerable distance from it, cutting off bends, perhaps to Second Lake, having first taken the course from the map with a compass, which was northeasterly, for safety. It was a wild wood-path, with a few tracks of oxen which had been driven over it, probably to some old camp clearing, for pasturage, mingled with the tracks of moose which had lately used it. We kept on steadily for about an hour without putting down our packs, occasionally winding around or climbing over a fallen tree, for the most part far out of sight and hearing of the river; till, after walking about three miles, we were glad to find that the path came to the river again at an old camp ground, where there was a small opening in the forest, at which we paused. Swiftly as the shallow and rocky river ran here, a continuous rapid with dancing waves, I saw, as I sat on the shore, a long string of sheldrakes, which something scared, run up the opposite side of the stream by me, with the same ease that they commonly did down it, just touching the surface of the waves, and getting an impulse from them as they flowed from under them; but they soon came back, driven by the Indian, who had fallen a little behind us, on account of the windings. He shot round a point just above, and came to land by us with considerable water in his canoe. He had found it, as he said, "very strong water," and had been obliged to land once before to empty out what he had taken in.

After this rough walking in the dark woods it was an agreeable change to glide down the rapid river in the canoe once more. This river, which was about the size of our Assabet (in Concord), though still very swift, was almost perfectly smooth here, and showed a very visible declivity, a regularly inclined plane, for several miles, like a mirror set a little aslant, on which we coasted down. This very obvious regular descent, particularly plain when I regarded the water-line against the shores, made a singular impression on me, which the swiftness of our motion probably enhanced, so that we seemed to be gliding down a much steeper declivity than we were, and that we could not save ourselves from rapids and falls if we should suddenly come to them. My companion did not perceive this slope, but I have a surveyor's eyes, and I satisfied myself that it was no ocular illusion. You could tell at a glance on approaching such a river, which way the water flowed, though you might perceive no motion. I observed the angle at which a level line would strike the surface, and calculated the amount of fall in a rod, which did not need to be remarkably great to produce this effect.

It was very exhilarating, and the perfection of travelling, quite unlike floating on our dead Concord River, the coasting down this inclined mirror, which was now and then gently winding, down a mountain, indeed, between two evergreen forests, edged with lofty dead white pines, sometimes slanted half-way over the stream, and destined soon to bridge it. I saw some monsters there, nearly destitute of branches, and scarcely diminishing in diameter for eighty or ninety feet.

Coming to falls and rapids, our easy progress was suddenly terminated. The Indian went along shore to inspect the water, while we climbed over the rocks, picking berries. The peculiar growth of blueberries on the tops of large rocks here made the impression of high land, and indeed this was the Height-of-land stream. When the Indian came back, he remarked, "You got to walk; ver strong water." So, taking out his canoe, he launched it again below the falls, and was soon out of sight. At such times, he would step into the canoe, take up his paddle, and, with an air of mystery, start off, looking far down stream, and keeping his own counsel, as if absorbing all the intelligence of forest and stream into himself; but I sometimes detected a little fun in his face, which could yield to my sympathetic smile, for he was thoroughly good-humored. We meanwhile scrambled along the shore with our packs, without any path. This was the last of *our* boating for the day.

The prevailing rock here was a kind of slate, standing on its edges, and my companion, who was recently from California, thought it exactly like that in which the gold is found, and said that if he had had a pan he would have liked to wash a little of the sand here.

When we reached the shore, the Indian appeared from out the woods on the opposite side, but on account of the roar of the water it was difficult to communicate with him. He kept along the shore westward to his canoe, while we stopped at the angle where the stream turned southward around the precipice. I again said to my companion, that we would keep along the shore and keep the Indian in sight. We started to do so, being close together, the Indian behind us having launched his canoe again, but just then I saw the latter, who had crossed to our side, forty or fifty rods behind, beckoning to me, and I called to my companion, who had just disappeared behind large rocks at the point of the precipice, three or four rods before me, on his way down the stream, that I was going to help the Indian a moment. I did so,—helped get the canoe over a fall, lying with my breast over a rock, and holding one end while he received it below,—and within ten or fifteen minutes at most I was back again at the point where the river turned southward, in order to catch up with my companion, while Polis glided down the river alone, parallel with me. But to my surprise, when I rounded the precipice, though the shore was bare of trees, not of rocks, for a quarter of a mile at least, my companion was not to be seen. It was as if he had sunk into the earth. This was the more unaccountable to me, because I knew that his feet were since our swamp walk very sore, and that he wished to keep with the party; and besides this was very bad walking, climbing over or about the rocks. I hastened along, hallooing and searching for him, thinking he might be concealed behind a rock, yet doubting if he had not taken the other side of the precipice, but the Indian had got along still faster in his canoe, till he was ar-

rested by the falls, about a quarter of a mile below.
He then landed, and said that we could go no farther
that night. The sun was setting, and on account of
falls and rapids we should be obliged to leave this
river and carry a good way into another farther east.
The first thing then was to find my companion, for I
was now very much alarmed about him, and I sent
the Indian along the shore down stream, which
began to be covered with unburnt wood again just
below the falls, while I searched backward about the
precipice which we had passed. The Indian showed
some unwillingness to exert himself, complaining
that he was very tired, in consequence of his day's
work, that it had strained him very much getting
down so many rapids alone; but he went off calling
somewhat like an owl. I remembered that my companion was near-sighted, and I feared that he had either fallen from the precipice, or fainted and sunk
down amid the rocks beneath it. I shouted and
searched above and below this precipice in the twilight till I could not see, expecting nothing less than
to find his body beneath it. For half an hour I anticipated and believed only the worst. I thought what
I should do the next day, if I did not find him, what I
could do in such a wilderness, and how his relatives
would feel, if I should return without him. I felt that
if he were really lost away from the river there, it
would be a desperate undertaking to find him; and
where were they who could help you? What would it

be to raise the country, where there were only two or three camps, twenty or thirty miles apart, and no road, and perhaps nobody at home? Yet we must try the harder, the less the prospect of success.

I rushed down from this precipice to the canoe in order to fire the Indian's gun, but found that my companion had the caps. I was still thinking of getting it off when the Indian returned. He had not found him, but he said that he had seen his tracks once or twice along the shore. This encouraged me very much. He objected to firing the gun, saying that if my companion heard it, which was not likely, on account of the roar of the stream, it would tempt him to come toward us, and he might break his neck in the dark. For the same reason we refrained from lighting a fire on the highest rock. I proposed that we should keep down the stream to the lake, or that I should go at any rate, but the Indian said, "No use, can't do anything in the dark; come morning, then we find 'em. No harm,—he make 'em camp. No bad animals here, no gristly bears, such as in California, where he's been,—warm night,—he well off as you and I." I considered that if he was well he could do without us. He had just lived eight years in California, and had plenty of experience with wild beasts and wilder men, was peculiarly accustomed to make journeys of great length, but if he were sick or dead, he was near where we were. The darkness in the woods was by this so thick that it alone decided the question. We must camp where we were. I knew that he had his knapsack, with blankets and matches, and if well, would fare no worse than we, except that he would have no supper nor society.

Thursday, July 30

I aroused the Indian early this morning to go in search of our companion, expecting to find him within a mile or two, farther down the stream. The Indian wanted his breakfast first, but I reminded him that my companion had had neither breakfast nor supper. We were obliged first to carry our canoe and baggage over into another stream, the main East Branch, about three fourths of a mile distant, for Webster Stream was no farther navigable. We went twice over this carry, and the dewy bushes wet us through like water up to the middle; I hallooed in a high key from time to time, though I had little expectation that I could be heard over the roar of the rapids, and moreover we were necessarily on the opposite side of the stream to him. In going over this portage the last time, the Indian, who was before me with the canoe on his head, stumbled and fell heavily once, and lay for a moment silent, as if in pain. I hastily stepped forward to help him, asking if he was much hurt, but after a moment's pause, without replying, he sprang up and went forward. He was all the way subject to taciturn fits, but they were harmless ones.

We had launched our canoe and gone but little way down the East Branch, when I heard an answering shout from my companion, and soon after saw him standing on a point where there was a clearing a quarter of a mile below, and the smoke of his fire was rising near by. Before I saw him I naturally shouted again and again, but the Indian curtly remarked, "He hears you," as if once was enough. It was just below the mouth of Webster Stream. When we arrived, he was smoking his pipe, and said that he had passed a pretty comfortable night, though it was rather cold, on account of the dew.

We all had good appetites for the breakfast which we made haste to cook here, and then, having partially dried our clothes, we glided swiftly down the winding stream toward Second Lake.

As the shores became flatter with frequent gravel and sand bars, and the stream more winding in the lower land near the lake, elms and ash trees made their appearance; also the wild yellow lily (*Lilium Canadense*), some of whose bulbs I collected for a soup. On some ridges the burnt land extended as far as the lake. This was a very beautiful lake, two or three miles long, with high mountains on the southwest side, the (as our Indian said) *Nerlumskeechticook,* i. e. Dead-Water Mountain. It appears to be the same called Carbuncle Mountain on the map. According to Polis, it extends in separate elevations all along this and the next lake, which is much larger. The lake, too, I think, is called by the same name, or perhaps with the addition of *gamoc* or *mooc*. The morning was a bright one, and perfectly still and serene, the lake as smooth as glass, we making the only ripples as we paddled into it. The dark mountains about it were seen through a glaucous mist, and the brilliant white stems of canoe-birches mingled with the other woods around it. The wood-thrush sang on the distant shore, and the laugh of some loons, sporting in a concealed western bay, as if inspired by the morning, came distinct over the lake to us, and, what was remarkable, the echo which ran round the lake was much louder than the original note; probably because, the loons being in a regularly curving bay under the mountain, we were exactly in the focus of many echoes, the sound being reflected like light from a concave mirror. The beauty of the scene may have been enhanced to our eyes by the fact that we had just come together again after a night of some anxiety.

It was not apparent where the outlet of this lake was, and while the Indian thought it was in one direction, I thought it was in another. He said, "I bet you fourpence it is there," but he still held on in my direction, which proved to be the right one. As we were approaching the outlet, it being still early in the forenoon, he suddenly exclaimed, "Moose! moose!"

and told us to be still. He put a cap on his gun, and standing up in the stern, rapidly pushed the canoe straight toward the shore and the moose. It was a cow-moose, about thirty rods off, standing in the water by the side of the outlet, partly behind some fallen timber and bushes, and at that distance she did not look very large. She was flapping her large ears, and from time to time poking off the flies with her nose from some part of her body. She did not appear much alarmed by our neighborhood, only occasionally turned her head and looked straight at us, and then gave her attention to the flies again. As we approached nearer, she got out of the water, stood higher and regarded us more suspiciously. Polis pushed the canoe steadily forward in the shallow water, and I for a moment forgot the moose in attending to some pretty rose-colored Polygonums just rising above the surface, but the canoe soon grounded in the mud eight or ten rods distant from the moose, and the Indian seized his gun and prepared to fire. After standing still a moment, she turned slowly, as usual, so as to expose her side, and he improved this moment to fire, over our heads. She thereupon moved off eight or ten rods at a moderate pace, across a shallow bay, to an old standing-place of hers, behind some fallen red maples, on the opposite shore, and there she stood still again a dozen or fourteen rods from us, while the Indian hastily loaded and fired twice at her, without her moving. My companion, who passed him his caps and bullets, said that Polis was as excited as a boy of fifteen, that his hand trembled, and he once put his ramrod back upside down. This was remarkable for so experienced a hunter. Perhaps he was anxious to make a good shot before us. The white hunter had told me that the Indians were not good shots, because they were excited, though he said that we had got a good hunter with us.

The Indian now pushed quickly and quietly back, and a long distance round, in order to get into the outlet,—for he had fired over the neck of a peninsula between it and the lake,—till we approached the place where the moose had stood, when he exclaimed, "She is a goner," and was surprised that we did not see her as soon as he did. There, to be sure, she lay perfectly dead, with her tongue hanging out, just where she had stood to receive the last shots, looking unexpectedly large and horse-like, and we saw where the bullets had scored the trees.

Using a tape, I found that the moose measured just six feet from the shoulder to the tip of the hoof, and was eight feet long as she lay. Some portions of the body, for a foot in diameter, were almost covered with flies, apparently the common fly of our woods, with a dark spot on the wing, and not the very large ones which occasionally pursued us in mid-stream, though both are called moose-flies.

Polis, preparing to skin the moose, asked me to help him find a stone on which to sharpen his large knife. It being all a flat alluvial ground where the moose had fallen, covered with red maples, &c., this was no easy matter; we searched far and wide, a long time, till at length I found a flat kind of slate-stone, and soon after he returned with a similar one, on which he soon made his knife very sharp.

While he was skinning the moose, I proceeded to ascertain what kind of fishes were to be found in the sluggish and muddy outlet. The greatest difficulty was to find a pole. It was almost impossible to find a slender, straight pole ten or twelve feet long in those woods. You might search half an hour in vain. They are commonly spruce, arbor-vitae, fir, &c., short, stout, and branchy, and do not make good fish-poles, even after you have patiently cut off all their tough and scraggy branches. The fishes were red perch and chivin.

The Indian having cut off a large piece of sirloin, the upper lip and the tongue, wrapped them in the hide, and placed them in the bottom of the canoe, observing that there was "one man," meaning the weight of one.

I cannot tell how many times we had to walk on account of falls or rapids. We were expecting all the while that the river would take a final leap and get to smooth water, but there was no improvement this forenoon. However, the carries were an agreeable variety. So surely as we stepped out of the canoe and stretched our legs we found ourselves in a blueberry and raspberry garden, each side of our rocky trail around the falls being lined with one or both. There was not a carry on the main East Branch where we did not find an abundance of both these berries, for these were the rockiest places, and partially cleared, such as these plants prefer, and there had been none to gather the finest before us.

In our three journeys over the carries, for we were obliged to go over the ground three times whenever the canoe was taken out, we did full justice to the berries, and they were just what we wanted to correct the effect of our hard bread and pork diet. Another name for making a portage would have been going a berrying.

We spent at least half the time in walking to-day, and the walking was as bad as usual, for the Indian being alone, commonly ran down far below the foot of the carries before he waited for us. The carry-paths themselves were more than usually indistinct, often the route being revealed only by the countless small holes in the fallen timber made by the tacks in the drivers' boots, or where there *was* a slight trail we did not find it. It was a tangled and perplexing thicket, through which we stumbled and threaded our way, and when we had finished a mile of it, our starting-point seemed far away. We were glad that we had not got to walk to Bangor along the banks of this river, which would be a journey of more than a hundred miles. Think of the denseness of the forest, the fallen trees and rocks, the windings of the river, the streams emptying in and the frequent swamps to be crossed. It made you shudder. Yet the Indian from time to time pointed out to us where he had thus crept along day after day when he was a boy of ten, and in a starving condition. He had been hunting far north of this with two grown Indians. The winter came on unexpectedly early, and the ice compelled them to leave their canoe at Grand Lake, and walk down the bank. They shouldered their furs and started for Oldtown. The snow was not deep enough for snow-shoes, or to cover the inequalities of the ground. Polis was soon too weak to carry any burden; but he managed to catch one otter. This was the most they all had to eat on this journey, and he remembered how good the yellow-lily roots were, made into a soup with the otter oil. He shared this food equally with the other two, but being so small he suffered much more than they. He waded through the Mattawamkeag at its mouth, when it was freezing cold and came up to his chin, and he, being very weak and emaciated, expected to be swept away. The first house which they reached was at Lincoln, and thereabouts they met a white teamster with supplies, who seeing their condition gave them as much of his load as they could eat. For six months after getting home he was very low, and did not expect to live, and was perhaps always the worse for it.

August 1

I caught two or three large red chivin (*Leuciscus pulchellus*) early this morning, within twenty feet of the camp, which, added to the moose-tongue, that had been left in the kettle boiling over night, and to our other stores, made a sumptuous breakfast. The Indian made us some hemlock tea instead of coffee, and we were not obliged to go as far as China for it; indeed, not quite so far as for the fish. This was tolerable, though he said it was not strong enough. It was interesting to see so simple a dish as a kettle of water with a handful of green hemlock sprigs in it, boiling over the huge fire in the open air, the leaves fast losing their lively green color, and know that it was for our breakfast.

We were glad to embark once more, and leave some of the mosquitoes behind. We had passed the *Wassataquoik* without perceiving it. This, according to the Indian, is the name of the main East Branch itself, and not properly applied to this small tributary alone, as on the maps.

We found that we had camped about a mile above Hunt's, which is on the east bank, and is the last house for those who ascend Ktaadn on this side.

* * *

Maples grew more and more numerous. It was lowering, and rained a little during the forenoon, and, as we expected a wetting, we stopped early and dined on the east side of a small expansion of the river, just above what are probably called Whetstone Falls, about a dozen miles below Hunt's. There were pretty fresh moose-tracks by the water-side. There were singular long ridges hereabouts, called "horse-backs," covered with ferns. My companion having lost his pipe asked the Indian if he could not make him one. "O yer," said he, and in a minute rolled up one of birch-bark, telling him to wet the bowl from time to time. Here also he left his gazette on a tree.

We carried round the falls just below, on the west side. The rocks were on their edges, and very sharp. The distance was about three fourths of a mile. When we had carried over one load, the Indian returned by the shore, and I by the path; and though I made no particular haste, I was nevertheless surprised to find him at the other end as soon as I. It was remarkable how easily he got along over the worst ground. He said to me, "I take canoe and you take the rest, suppose you can keep along with me?" I thought that he meant, that while he ran down the rapids I should keep along the shore, and be ready to assist him from time to time, as I had done before; but as the walking would be very bad, I answered, "I suppose you will go too fast for me, but I will try." But

I was to go by the path, he said. This I thought would
not help the matter, I should have so far to go to get
to the river-side when he wanted me. But neither
was this what he meant. He was proposing a race
over the carry, and asked me if I thought I could keep
along with him by the same path, adding that I must
be pretty smart to do it. As his load, the canoe, would
be much the heaviest and bulkiest, though the sim-
plest, I thought that I ought to be able to do it, and
said that I would try. So I proceeded to gather up the
gun, axe, paddle, kettle, frying-pan, plates, dippers,
carpets, &c., &c., and while I was thus engaged he
threw me his cow-hide boots. "What, are these in the
bargain?" I asked. "O yer," said he; but before I could
make a bundle of my load I saw him disappearing
over a hill with the canoe on his head; so, hastily
scraping the various articles together, I started on the
run, and immediately went by him in the bushes, but
I had no sooner left him out of sight in a rocky hollow, than the greasy plates, dippers, &c., took to
themselves wings, and while I was employed in gathering them up again, he went by me; but hastily
pressing the sooty kettle to my side, I started once
more, and soon passing him again, I saw him no
more on the carry. I do not mention this as anything
of a feat, for it was but poor running on my part, and
he was obliged to move with great caution for fear
of breaking his canoe as well as his neck. When
he made his appearance, puffing and panting like

myself, in answer to my inquiries where he had been, he said, "Locks (rocks) cut 'em feet," and laughing added, "O, me love to play sometimes." He said that he and his companions when they came to carries several miles long used to try who would get over first; each perhaps with a canoe on his head. I bore the sign of the kettle on my brown linen sack for the rest of the voyage.

We camped about two miles below Nickertow, on the south side of the West Branch, covering with fresh twigs the withered bed of a former traveller, and feeling that we were now in a settled country, especially when in the evening we heard an ox sneeze in its wild pasture across the river. Wherever you land along the frequented part of the river, you have not far to go to find these sites of temporary inns, the withered bed of flattened twigs, the charred sticks, and perhaps the tent-poles. And not long since, similar beds were spread along the Connecticut, the Hudson, and the Delaware, and longer still ago, by the Thames and Seine, and they now help to make the soil where private and public gardens, mansions and palaces are. We could not get fir twigs for our bed here, and the spruce was harsh in comparison, having more twig in proportion to its leaf, but we improved it somewhat with hemlock. The Indian remarked as before, "Must have hard wood to cook moose-meat," as if that were a maxim, and pro-

ceeded to get it. My companion cooked some in California fashion, winding a long string of the meat
round a stick and slowly turning it in his hand before
the fire. It was very good. But the Indian not approv-
ing of the mode, or because he was not allowed to
cook it his own way, would not taste it.

Sunday, August 2,—

Was a cloudy and unpromising morning. One of
us observed to the Indian, "You did not stretch your
moose-hide last night, did you, Mr. Polis?" Whereat
he replied, in a tone of surprise, though perhaps not
of ill humor: "What you ask me that question for?
Suppose I stretch 'em, you see 'em. May be your
way talking, may be all right, no Indian way." I had
observed that he did not wish to answer the same
question more than once, and was often silent when
it was put again for the sake of certainty, as if he
were moody. Not that he was incommunicative, for
he frequently commenced a long-winded narrative
of his own accord,—repeated at length the tradition
of some old battle, or some passage in the recent
history of his tribe in which he had acted a prominent part, from time to time drawing a long breath,
and resuming the thread of his tale, with the true
story-teller's leisureliness, perhaps after shooting a
rapid,—prefacing with "we-ll-by-by," &c., as he paddled along. Especially after the day's work was over,
and he had put himself in posture for the night,

he would be unexpectedly sociable, exhibit even the *bonhommie* of a Frenchman, and we would fall asleep before he got through his periods.

Nickertow is called eleven miles from Matta-wamkeag by the river. Our camp was, therefore, about nine miles from the latter place.

The small river emptying in at Lincoln is the Matanawcook, which also, we noticed, was the name of a steamer moored there. So we paddled and floated along, looking into the mouths of rivers. When passing the Mohawk Rips, or, as the Indian called them, "Mohog lips," four or five miles below Lincoln, he told us at length the story of a fight between his tribe and the Mohawks there, anciently,— how the latter were overcome by stratagem, the Penobscots using concealed knives,—but they could not for a long time kill the Mohawk chief, who was a very large and strong man, though he was attacked by several canoes at once, when swimming alone in the river.

From time to time we met Indians in their canoes, going up river. Our man did not commonly approach them, but exchanged a few words with them at a distance in his tongue. These were the first Indians we had met since leaving the *Umbazookskus*.

At Piscataquis Falls, just above the river of that name, we walked over the wooden railroad on the eastern shore, about one and a half miles long, while

the Indian glided down the rapids. The steamer from
Oldtown stops here, and passengers take a new boat
above. Piscataquis, whose mouth we here passed,
means "branch." It is obstructed by falls at its mouth,
but can be navigated with bateaux or canoes above
through a settled country, even to the neighborhood
of Moosehead Lake, and we had thought at first of
going that way. We were not obliged to get out of the
canoe after this on account of falls or rapids, nor,
indeed, was it quite necessary here. We took less
notice of the scenery to-day, because we were in
quite a settled country. The river became broad and
sluggish, and we saw a blue heron winging its way
slowly down the stream before us.

[The Indian] had previously complimented me on
my paddling, saying that I paddled "just like anybody," giving me an Indian name which meant "great
paddler." When off this stream he said to me, who sat
in the bows, "Me teach you paddle." So turning toward the shore he got out, came forward and placed
my hands as he wished. He placed one of them quite
outside the boat, and the other parallel with the first,
grasping the paddle near the end, not over the flat extremity, and told me to slide it back and forth on the
side of the canoe. This, I found, was a great improvement which I had not thought of, saving me the labor
of lifting the paddle each time, and I wondered that

he had not suggested it before. It is true, before our baggage was reduced we had been obliged to sit with our legs drawn up, and our knees above the side of the canoe, which would have prevented our paddling thus, or perhaps he was afraid of wearing out his canoe, by constant friction on the side.

I told him that I had been accustomed to sit in the stern, and lifting my paddle at each stroke, getting a pry on the side each time, and I still paddled partly as if in the stern. He then wanted to see me paddle in the stern. So, changing paddles, for he had the longer and better one, and turning end for end, he sitting flat on the bottom and I on the crossbar, he began to paddle very hard, trying to turn the canoe, looking over his shoulder and laughing, but finding it in vain he relaxed his efforts, though we still sped along a mile or two very swiftly. He said that he had no fault to find with my paddling in the stern, but I complained that he did not paddle according to his own directions in the bows.

Opposite the Sunkhaze is the main boom of the Penobscot, where the logs from far up the river are collected and assorted.

As we drew near to Oldtown I asked Polis if he was not glad to get home again; but there was no relenting to his wildness, and he said, "It makes no difference to me where I am." Such is the Indian's pretence always.

We approached the Indian Island through the narrow strait called "Cook." He said, "I 'xpect we take in some water there, river so high,—never see it so high at this season. Very rough water there, but short; swamp steamboat once. Don't you paddle till I tell you, then you paddle right along." It was a very short rapid. When we were in the midst of it he shouted "paddle," and we shot through without taking in a drop.

Soon after the Indian houses came in sight, but I could not at first tell my companion which of two or three large white ones was our guide's. He said it was the one with blinds.

We landed opposite his door at about four in the afternoon, having come some forty miles this day. From the Piscataquis we had come remarkably and unaccountably quick, probably as fast as the stage on the bank, though the last dozen miles was dead water.

Polis wanted to sell us his canoe, said it would last seven or eight years, or with care, perhaps ten; but we were not ready to buy it.

We stopped for an hour at his house, where my companion shaved with his razor, which he pronounced in very good condition. Mrs. P. wore a hat and had a silver brooch on her breast, but she was not introduced to us. The house was roomy and neat. A large new map of Oldtown and the Indian Island hung on the wall, and a clock opposite to it. Wishing to know when the cars left Oldtown, Polis's son brought one of the last Bangor papers, which I saw was directed to "Joseph Polis," from the office.

This was the last that I saw of Joe Polis. We took the last train, and reached Bangor that night.

Cape Cod

Cape Cod

The Shipwreck

WISHING TO GET a better view than I had yet had of the ocean, which, we are told, covers more than two thirds of the globe, but of which a man who lives a few miles inland may never see any trace, more than of another world, I made a visit to Cape Cod in October, 1849, another the succeeding June, and another to Truro in July, 1855; the first and last time with a single companion, the second time alone. I have spent, in all, about three weeks on the Cape; walked from Eastham to Provincetown twice on the Atlantic side, and once on the Bay side also, excepting four or five miles, and crossed the Cape half a dozen times on my way; but having come so fresh to the sea, I have got but little salted. My readers must expect only so much saltness as the land breeze acquires from blowing over an arm of the sea, or is tasted on the windows and the bark of trees twenty miles inland, after September gales. I have been accustomed to make excursions to the ponds within ten miles of Concord, but latterly I have extended my excursions to the sea-shore.

* * *

Cape Cod is the bared and bended arm of Massachusetts: the shoulder is at Buzzard's Bay; the ebow,
or crazy-bone, at Cape Mallebarre; the wrist at Truro;
and the sandy fist at Provincetown,—behind which
the State stands on her guard, with her back to the
Green Mountains, and her feet planted on the floor
of the ocean, like an athlete protecting her Bay,—
boxing with northeast storms, and, ever and anon,
heaving up her Atlantic adversary from the lap of
earth,—ready to thrust forward her other fist, which
keeps guard the while upon her breast at Cape Ann.

On studying the map, I saw that there must be an
uninterrupted beach on the east or outside of the
fore-arm of the Cape, more than thirty miles from the
general line of the coast, which would afford a good
sea view, but that, on account of an opening in the
beach, forming the entrance to Nauset Harbor, in
Orleans, I must strike it in Eastham, if I approached
it by land, and probably I could walk thence straight
to Race Point, about twenty-eight miles, and not
meet with any obstruction.

We left Concord, Massachusetts, on Tuesday, October 9th, 1849. On reaching Boston, we found that
the Provincetown steamer, which should have got in
the day before, had not yet arrived, on account of a
violent storm; and, as we noticed in the streets a
handbill headed, "Death! one hundred and forty-five
lives lost at Cohasset," we decided to go by way of
Cohasset. We found many Irish in the cars, going to

identify bodies and to sympathize with the survivors, and also to attend the funeral which was to take place in the afternoon;—and when we arrived at Cohasset, it appeared that nearly all the passengers were bound for the beach, which was about a mile distant, and many other persons were flocking in from the neighboring country. There were several hundreds of them streaming off over Cohasset common in that direction, some on foot and some in wagons,—and among them were some sportsmen in their hunting-jackets, with their guns, and game-bags, and dogs. As we passed the graveyard we saw a large hole, like a cellar, freshly dug there, and, just before reaching the shore, by a pleasantly winding and rocky road, we met several hay-riggings and farm-wagons coming away toward the meeting-house, each loaded with three large, rough deal boxes. We did not need to ask what was in them. The owners of the wagons were made the undertakers. Many horses in carriages were fastened to the fences near the shore, and, for a mile or more, up and down, the beach was covered with people looking out for bodies, and examining the fragments of the wreck. There was a small island called Brook Island, with a hut on it, lying just off the shore. This is said to be the rockiest shore in Massachusetts, from Nantasket to Scituate,—hard sienitic rocks, which the waves have laid bare, but have not been able to crumble. It has been the scene of many a shipwreck.

The brig *St. John,* from Galway, Ireland, laden with emigrants, was wrecked on Sunday morning; it was now Tuesday morning, and the sea was still breaking violently on the rocks. There were eighteen or twenty of the same large boxes that I have mentioned, lying on a green hill-side, a few rods from the water, and surrounded by a crowd. The bodies which had been recovered, twenty-seven or eight in all, had been collected there. Some were rapidly nailing down the lids, others were carting the boxes away, and others were lifting the lids, which were yet loose, and peeping under the cloths, for each body, with such rags as still adhered to it, was covered loosely with a white sheet. I witnessed no signs of grief, but there was a sober despatch of business which was affecting. One man was seeking to identify a particular body, and one undertaker or carpenter was calling to another to know in what box a certain child was put. I saw many marble feet and matted heads as the cloths were raised, and one livid, swollen, and mangled body of a drowned girl,—who probably had intended to go out to service in some American family,—to which some rags still adhered, with a string, half concealed by the flesh, about its swollen neck; the coiled-up wreck of a human hulk, gashed by the rocks or fishes, so that the bone and muscle were exposed, but quite bloodless,—merely red and white,—with wide-open and staring eyes, yet lustreless, dead-lights; or like the cabin windows of a stranded vessel, filled with sand.

* * *

We turned from this and walked along the rocky shore. In the first cove were strewn what seemed the fragments of a vessel, in small pieces mixed with sand and sea-weed, and great quantities of feathers; but it looked so old and rusty, that I at first took it to be some old wreck which had lain there many years. I even thought of Captain Kidd, and that the feathers were those which sea-fowl had cast there; and per- haps there might be some tradition about it in the neighborhood. I asked a sailor if that was the *St. John*. He said it was. I asked him where she struck. He pointed to a rock in front of us, a mile from the shore, called the Grampus Rock, and added:—

"You can see a part of her now sticking up; it looks like a small boat."

I saw it. It was thought to be held by the chain-ca- bles and the anchors. I asked if the bodies which I saw were all that were drowned.

"Not a quarter of them," said he.

"Where are the rest?"

"Most of them right underneath that piece you see."

It appeared to us that there was enough rubbish to make the wreck of a large vessel in this cove alone, and that it would take many days to cart it off. It was several feet deep, and here and there was a bon- net or a jacket on it. In the very midst of the crowd about this wreck, there were men with carts busily collecting the sea-weed which the storm had cast up, and conveying it beyond the reach of the tide, though they were often obliged to separate fragments of clothing from it, and they might at any moment have found a human body under it. Drown who might, they did not forget that this weed was a valuable manure. This shipwreck had not produced a visible vibration in the fabric of society.

On the whole, it was not so impressive a scene as I might have expected. If I had found one body cast upon the beach in some lonely place, it would have affected me more. I sympathized rather with the winds and waves, as if to toss and mangle these poor human bodies was the order of the day. If this was the law of Nature, why waste any time in awe or pity? If the last day were come, we should not think so much about the separation of friends or the blighted prospects of individuals. I saw that corpses might be multiplied, as on the field of battle, till they no longer affected us in any degree, as exceptions to the common lot of humanity. Take all the graveyards together, they are always the majority. It is the individual and private that demands our sympathy. A man can attend but one funeral in the course of his life, can behold but one corpse. Yet I saw that the inhabitants of the shore would be not a little affected by this event. They would watch there many days and nights for the sea to give up its dead, and their imaginations and sympathies would supply the place of mourners far away, who as yet knew not of the wreck. Many days after this, something white was seen floating on the water by one who was sauntering on the beach. It was approached in a boat, and found to be the body of a woman, which had risen in an upright position, whose white cap was blown back with the wind. I saw that the beauty of the shore itself was wrecked for many a lonely walker there, until he could perceive, at last, how its beauty was enhanced by wrecks like this, and it acquired thus a rarer and sublimer beauty still.

Why care for these dead bodies? They really have no friends but the worms or fishes. Their owners were coming to the New World, as Columbus and the Pilgrims did,—they were within a mile of its shores; but, before they could reach it, they emigrated to a newer world than ever Columbus dreamed of, yet one of whose existence we believe that there is far more universal and convincing evidence—though it has not yet been discovered by science—than Columbus had of this; not merely mariners' tales and some paltry drift-wood and sea-weed, but a continual drift and instinct to all our shores. I saw their empty hulks that came to land; but they themselves, meanwhile, were cast upon some shore yet further west, toward which we are all tending, and which we shall reach at last, it may be through storm and darkness, as they did. No doubt, we have reason to thank God

that they have not been "shipwrecked into life again."
The mariner who makes the safest port in Heaven,
perchance, seems to his friends on earth to be shipwrecked, for they deem Boston Harbor the better
place; though perhaps invisible to them, a skilful pilot
comes to meet him, and the fairest and balmiest
gales blow off that coast, his good ship makes the
land in halcyon days, and he kisses the shore in rap-
ture there, while his old hulk tosses in the surf here.
It is hard to part with one's body, but, no doubt, it
is easy enough to do without it when once it is gone.
All their plans and hopes burst like a bubble! Infants
by the score dashed on the rocks by the enraged Atlantic Ocean! No, no! If the St. John did not make her
port here, she has been telegraphed there. The
strongest wind cannot stagger a Spirit; it is a Spirit's
breath. A just man's purpose cannot be split on any
Grampus or material rock, but itself will split rocks
till it succeeds.

I saw in Cohasset, separated from the sea only by
a narrow beach, a handsome but shallow lake of
some four hundred acres, which, I was told, the sea
had tossed over the beach in a great storm in the
spring, and, after the alewives had passed into it, it
had stopped up its outlet, and now the alewives were
dying by thousands, and the inhabitants were appre-
hending a pestilence as the water evaporated. It had
five rocky islets in it.

This rocky shore is called Pleasant Cove, on some maps; on the map of Cohasset, that name appears to be confined to the particular cove where I saw the wreck of the *St. John*. The ocean did not look, now, as if any were ever shipwrecked in it; it was not grand and sublime, but beautiful as a lake. Not a vestige of a wreck was visible, nor could I believe that the bones of many a shipwrecked man were buried in that pure sand. But to go on with our first excursion.

Stage-Coach Views

AFTER SPENDING the night in Bridgewater, and picking up a few arrow-heads there in the morning, we took the cars for Sandwich, where we arrived before noon. This was the terminus of the "Cape Cod Railroad," though it is but the beginning of the Cape. As it rained hard, with driving mists, and there was no sign of its holding up, we here took that almost obsolete conveyance, the stage, for "as far as it went that day," as we told the driver. We had forgotten how far a stage could go in a day, but we were told that the Cape roads were very "heavy," though they added that, being of sand, the rain would improve them. This coach was an exceedingly narrow one, but as there was a slight spherical excess over two on a seat, the driver waited till nine passengers had got in, without taking the measure of any of them, and then shut the door after two or three ineffectual slams, as if the fault were all in the hinges or the latch,—while we timed our inspirations and expirations so as to assist him.

We were now fairly on the Cape, which extends from Sandwich eastward thirty-five miles, and thence north and north-west thirty more, in all sixty-five, and has an average breadth of about five miles. In the interior it rises to the height of two hundred, and sometimes perhaps three hundred feet above the level of the sea. According to Hitchcock, the geologist of the State, it is composed almost entirely of sand, even to the depth of three hundred feet in some places, though there is probably a concealed core of rock a little beneath the surface, and it is of diluvian origin, excepting a small portion at the extremity and elsewhere along the shores, which is alluvial.

Our route was along the Bay side, through Barnstable, Yarmouth, Dennis, and Brewster, to Orleans, with a range of low hills on our right, running down the Cape. The weather was not favorable for wayside views, but we made the most of such glimpses of land and water as we could get through the rain. The country was, for the most part, bare, or with only a little scrubby wood left on the hills. We noticed in Yarmouth—and, if I do not mistake, in Dennis— large tracts where pitch-pines were planted four or five years before. They were in rows, as they appeared when we were abreast of them, and, excepting that there were extensive vacant spaces, seemed to be doing remarkably well. This, we were told, was the only use to which such tracts could be profitably put. Every higher eminence had a pole set up on it, with an old storm-coat or sail tied to it, for a signal, that those on the south side of the Cape, for instance, might know when the Boston packets had arrived on the north. It appeared as if this use must absorb the greater part of the old clothes of the Cape, leaving but few rags for the peddlers. The wind-mills on the hills,—large weather-stained octagonal structures,—and the salt-works scattered all along the shore, with their long rows of vats resting on piles driven into the marsh, their low, turtle-like roofs, and their slighter wind-mills, were novel and interesting objects to an inlander. The sand by the road-side was partially covered with bunches of a moss-like plant, *Hudsonia tomentosa,* which a woman in the stage told us was called "poverty grass," because it grew where nothing else would.

I was struck by the pleasant equality which reigned among the stage company, and their broad and invulnerable good humor. They were what is called free and easy, and met one another to advantage, as men who had, at length, learned how to live. They appeared to know each other when they were strangers, they were so simple and downright. They were well met, in an unusual sense, that is, they met as well as they could meet, and did not seem to be troubled with any impediment. They were not afraid nor ashamed of one another, but were contented to make just such a company as the ingredients allowed. It was evident that the same foolish respect was not here claimed, for mere wealth and station, that is in many parts of New England; yet some of them were the "first people," as they are called, of the various towns through which we passed. Retired sea-captains, in easy circumstances, who talked of farming as sea-captains are wont; an erect, respectable, and trustworthy-looking man, in his wrapper, some of the salt of the earth, who had formerly been the salt of the sea; or a more courtly gentleman, who, perchance, had been a representative to the General Court in his day; or a broad, red-faced Cape Cod man, who had seen too many storms to be easily irritated; or a fisherman's wife, who had been waiting a week for a coaster to leave Boston, and had at length come by the cars.

We passed through the village of Suet, in Dennis, on Suet and Quivet Necks, of which it is said, "when compared with Nobscusset,"—we had a misty recollection of having passed through, or near to, the latter,—"it may be denominated a pleasant village; but, in comparison with the village of Sandwich, there is little or no beauty in it." However, we liked Dennis well, better than any town we had seen on the Cape, it was so novel, and, in that stormy day, so sublimely dreary.

Captain John Sears, of Suet, was the first person in this country who obtained pure marine salt by solar evaporation alone; though it had long been made in a similar way on the coast of France, and elsewhere.

This was in the year 1776, at which time, on account of the war, salt was scarce and dear. The Historical Collections contain an interesting account of his experiments, which we read when we first saw the roofs of the salt-works. Barnstable county is the most favorable locality for these works on our northern coast,—there is so little fresh water here emptying into ocean. Quite recently there were about two millions of dollars invested in this business here. But now the Cape is unable to compete with the importers of salt and the manufacturers of it at the West, and, accordingly, her salt-works are fast going to decay. From making salt, they turn to fishing more than ever. The Gazetteer will uniformly tell you, under the head of each town, how many go a-fishing, and the value of the fish and oil taken, how much salt is made and used, how many are engaged in the coasting trade, how many in manufacturing palm-leaf hats, leather, boots, shoes, and tinware, and then it has done, and leaves you to imagine the more truly domestic manufacturers which are nearly the same all the world over.

Late in the afternoon, we rode through Brewster, so named after Elder Brewster, for fear he would be forgotten else. Who has not heard of Elder Brewster? Who knows who he was? This appeared to be the modern-built town of the Cape, the favorite residence of retired sea-captains. It is said that "there are more masters and mates of vessels which sail on

.foreign voyages belonging to this place than to any other town in the country."

At length, we stopped for the night at Higgins's tavern, in Orleans, feeling very much as if we were on a sand-bar in the ocean, and not knowing whether we should see land or water ahead when the mist cleared away. We here overtook two Italian boys, who had waded thus far down the Cape through the sand, with their organs on their backs, and were going on to Provincetown. What a hard lot, we thought, if the Provincetown people should shut their doors against them! Whose yard would they go to next? Yet we concluded that they had chosen wisely to come here, where other music than that of the surf must be rare. Thus the great civilizer sends out its emissaries, sooner or later, to every sandy cape and lighthouse of the New World which the census-taker visits, and summons the savage there to surrender.

The Wellfleet Oysterman

HAVING WALKED about eight miles since we struck the beach, and passed the boundary between Wellfleet and Truro, a stone post in the sand,—for even this sand comes under the jurisdiction of one town or another,—we turned inland over barren hills and valleys, whither the sea, for some reason, did not follow us, and, tracing up a Hollow, discovered two or three sober-looking houses within half a mile, uncommonly near the eastern coast.

These houses were on the shores of a chain of ponds, seven in number, the source of a small stream called Herring River, which empties into the Bay. There are many Herring Rivers on the Cape; they will, perhaps, be more numerous than herrings soon. We knocked at the door of the first house, but its inhabitants were all gone away. In the mean while, we saw the occupants of the next one looking out the window at us, and before we reached it an old woman came out and fastened the door of her bulk-head, and went in again. Nevertheless, we did not hesitate to knock at her door, when a grizzly-looking man appeared, whom we took to be sixty or seventy years old. He asked us, at first, suspiciously, where we were from, and what our business was; to which we returned plain answers.

"How far is Concord from Boston?" he inquired.

"Twenty miles by railroad."

"Twenty miles by railroad," he repeated.

"Did n't you ever hear of Concord of Revolutionary fame?"

"Did n't I ever hear of Concord? Why, I heard the guns fire at the battle of Bunker Hill. (They hear the sound of heavy cannon across the Bay.) I am almost ninety; I am eighty-eight year old. I was fourteen year old at the time of Concord Fight,—and where were you then?"

We were obliged to confess that we were not in the fight.

"Well, walk in, we'll leave it to the women," said he.

So we walked in, surprised, and sat down, an old woman taking our hats and bundles, and the old man continued, drawing up to the large, old-fashioned fireplace,—

"I am a poor good-for-nothing crittur, as Isaiah says; I am all broken down this year. I am under petticoat government here."

The family consisted of the old man, his wife, and his daughter, who appeared nearly as old as her mother, a fool, her son (a brutish-looking, middle-aged man, with a prominent lower face, who was standing by the hearth when we entered, but immediately went out), and a little boy of ten.

While my companion talked with the women, I talked with the old man. They said that he was old and foolish, but he was evidently too knowing for them.

"These women," said he to me, "are both of them poor good-for-nothing critturs. This one is my wife. I married her sixty-four years ago. She is eighty-four years old, and as deaf as an adder, and the other is not much better."

He thought well of the Bible, or at least he *spoke* well, and did not *think* ill, of it, for that would not have been prudent for a man of his age. He said that he had read it attentively for many years, and he had much of it at his tongue's end. He seemed deeply impressed with a sense of his own nothingness, and would repeatedly exclaim,—

"I am a nothing. What I gather from my Bible is just this: that man is a poor good-for-nothing crittur, and everything is just as God sees fit and disposes."

"May I ask your name?" I said.

"Yes," he answered, "I am not ashamed to tell my name. My name is——. My great-grandfather came over from England and settled here."

He was an old Wellfleet oysterman, who had acquired a competency in that business, and had sons still engaged in it.

Nearly all the oyster shops and stands in Massa-

chusetts, I am told, are supplied and kept by natives
of Wellfleet, and a part of this town is still called
Billingsgate from the oysters having been formerly
planted there; but the native oysters are said to have
died in 1770. Various causes are assigned for this,
such as a ground frost, the carcasses of black-fish,
kept to rot in the harbor, and the like, but the most
common account of the matter is,—and I find that a
similar superstition with regard to the disappearance
of fishes exists almost everywhere,—that when Wellfleet began to quarrel with the neighboring towns
about the right to gather them, yellow specks appeared in them, and Providence caused them to dis-
appear. A few years ago sixty thousand bushels were
annually brought from the South and planted in the
harbor of Wellfleet till they attained "the proper rel-
ish of Billingsgate"; but now they are imported commonly full-grown, and laid down near their markets,
at Boston and elsewhere, where the water, being a
mixture of salt and fresh, suits them better. The business was said to be still good and improving.

The old man said that the oysters were liable to
freeze in the winter, if planted too high; but if it were
not "so cold as to strain their eyes" they were not
injured. The inhabitants of New Brunswick have
noticed that "ice will not form over an oyster-bed,
unless the cold is very intense indeed, and when the
bays are frozen over the oyster-beds are easily discovered by the water above them remaining unfrozen, or

as the French residents say, *degèle*." Our host said
that they kept them in cellars all winter.

"Without anything to eat or drink?" I asked.

"Without anything to eat or drink," he answered.

"Can the oysters move?"

"Just as much as my shoe."

But when I caught him saying that they "bedded
themselves down in the sand, flat side up, round side
down," I told him that my shoe could not do that,
without the aid of my foot in it; at which he said that
they merely settled down as they grew; if put down in
a square they would be found so; but the clam could
move quite fast.

When I asked what they did with all that barren-
looking land, where I saw so few cultivated fields,—
"Nothing," he said.

"Then why fence your fields?"

"To keep the sand from blowing and covering up
the whole."

"The yellow sand," he said, "has some life in it, but
the white little or none."

When, in answer to his questions, I told him that
I was a surveyor, he said that they who surveyed his
farm were accustomed, where the ground was uneven, to loop up each chain as high as their elbows;
that was the allowance they made, and he wished to
know if I could tell him why they did not come out
according to his deed, or twice alike. He seemed to

have more respect for surveyors of the old school, which I did not wonder at. "King George the Third," said he, "laid out a road four rods wide and straight the whole length of the Cape," but where it was now he could not tell.

He gave us to taste what he called the Summer Sweeting, a pleasant apple which he raised, and frequently grafted from, but had never seen growing elsewhere, except once,—three trees on Newfoundland, or at the Bay of Chaleur, I forget which, as he was sailing by. He was sure that he could tell the tree at a distance.

At length the fool, whom my companion called the wizard, came in, muttering between his teeth, "Damn book-pedlers,—all the time talking about books. Better do something. Damn 'em. I'll shoot 'em. Got a doctor down here. Damn him, I'll get a gun and shoot him"; never once holding up his head. Whereat the old man stood up and said in a loud voice, as if he was accustomed to command, and this was not the first time he had been obliged to exert his authority there: "John, go sit down, mind your business,—we've heard you talk before,—precious little you'll do,—your bark is worse than your bite."

This was the merriest old man that we had ever seen, and one of the best preserved. His style of conversation was coarse and plain enough to have suited

Rabelais. He would have made a good Panurge. Or rather he was a sober Silenus, and we were the boys Chromis and Mnasilus, who listened to his story.

> Not by Haemonian hills the Thracian bard,
> Nor awful Phoebus was on Pindus heard
> With deeper silence or with more regard.

There was a strange mingling of past and present in his conversation, for he had lived under King George, and might have remembered when Napoleon and the moderns generally were born. He said that one day, when the troubles between the Colonies and the mother country first broke out, as he, a boy of fifteen, was pitching hay out of a cart, one Doane, an old Tory, who was talking with his father, a good Whig, said to him, "Why, Uncle Bill, you might as well undertake to pitch that pond into the ocean with a pitchfork, as for the Colonies to undertake to gain their independence." He remembered well General Washington, and how he rode his horse along the streets of Boston, and he stood up to show us how he looked.

"He was a r—a—ther large and portly-looking man, a manly and resolute-looking officer, with a pretty good leg as he sat on his horse."—"There, I'll tell you, this was the way with Washington." Then he jumped up again, and bowed gracefully to right and left, making show as if he were waving his hat. Said he, *"That* was Washington."

* * *

He told us the story of the wreck of the Franklin, which took place there the previous spring: how a boy came to his house early in the morning to know whose boat that was by the shore, for there was a vessel in distress, and he, being an old man, first ate his breakfast, and then walked over to the top of the hill by the shore, and sat down there, having found a comfortable seat, to see the ship wrecked. She was on the bar, only a quarter of a mile from him, and still nearer to the men on the beach, who had got a boat ready, but could render no assistance on account of the breakers, for there was a pretty high sea running. There were the passengers all crowded together in the forward part of the ship, and some were getting out of the cabin windows and were drawn on deck by the others.

"I saw the captain get out his boat," said he; "he had one little one; and then they jumped into it one after another, down as straight as an arrow. I counted them. There were nine. One was a woman, and she jumped as straight as any of them. Then they shoved off. The sea took them back, one wave went over them, and when they came up there were six still clinging to the boat; I counted them. The next wave turned the boat bottom upward, and emptied them all out. None of them ever came ashore alive. There were the rest of them all crowded together on the forecastle, the other parts of the ship being under water. They had seen all that happened to the boat.

At length a heavy sea separated the forecastle from the rest of the wreck, and set it inside of the worst breaker, and the boat was able to reach them, and it saved all that were left, but one woman."

At length the little boy, who had a seat quite in the chimney-corner, took off his stockings and shoes, warmed his feet, and having had his sore leg freshly salved, went off to bed; then the fool made bare his knotty-looking feet and legs, and followed him; and finally the old man exposed his calves also to our gaze. We had never had the good fortune to see an old man's legs before, and were surprised to find them fair and plump as an infant's, and we thought that he took a pride in exhibiting them. He then proceeded to make preparations for retiring, discoursing meanwhile with Panurgic plainness of speech on the ills to which old humanity is subject. We were a rare haul for him. He could commonly get none but ministers to talk to, though sometimes ten of them at once, and he was glad to meet some of the laity at leisure. The evening was not long enough for him.

Before sunrise the next morning they let us out again, and I ran over to the beach to see the sun come out of the ocean. The old woman of eighty-four winters was already out in the cold morning wind, bare-headed, tripping about like a young girl, and driving up the cow to milk. She got the breakfast with

despatch, and without noise or bustle; and meanwhile the old man resumed his stories, standing
before us, who were sitting, with his back to the
chimney, and ejecting his tobacco-juice right and left
into the fire behind him, without regard to the various dishes which were there preparing. At breakfast
we had eels, buttermilk cake, cold bread, green
beans, doughnuts, and tea. The old man talked a
steady stream; and when his wife told him he had
better eat his breakfast, he said: "Don't hurry me; I
have lived too long to be hurried." I ate of the apple-
sauce and the doughnuts, which I thought had sus-
tained the least detriment from the old man's shots,
but my companion refused the apple-sauce, and ate
of the hot cake and green beans, which had appeared
to him to occupy the safest part of the hearth. But on
comparing notes afterward, I told him that the buttermilk cake was particularly exposed, and I saw how
it suffered repeatedly, and therefore I avoided it; but
he declared that, however that might be, he witnessed that the apple-sauce was seriously injured,
and had therefore declined that. After breakfast we
looked at his clock, which was out of order, and oiled
it with some "hen's grease," for want of sweet oil, for
he scarcely could believe that we were not tinkers or
pedlers; meanwhile he told a story about visions,
which had reference to a crack in the clock-case
made by frost one night. He was curious to know to
what religious sect we belonged. He said that he had

been to hear thirteen kinds of preaching in one month, when he was young, but he did not join any of them,—he stuck to his Bible. There was nothing like any of them in his Bible. While I was shaving in the next room, I heard him ask my companion to what sect he belonged, to which he answered:

"O, I belong to the Universal Brotherhood."

"What's that?" he asked, "Sons o' Temperance?"

Finally, filling our pockets with doughnuts, which he was pleased to find that we called by the same name that he did, and paying for our entertainment, we took our departure; but he followed us out of doors, and made us tell him the names of the vegetables which he had raised from seeds that came out of the Franklin. They were cabbage, broccoli, and parsley. As I had asked him the names of so many things, he tried me in turn with all the plants which grew in his garden, both wild and cultivated. It was about half an acre, which he cultivated wholly himself. Besides the common garden vegetables, there were Yellow-Dock, Lemon Balm, Hyssop, Gill-go-over-the-ground, Mouse-ear, Chick-weed, Roman Wormwood, Elecampane, and other plants. As we stood there, I saw a fish-hawk stoop to pick a fish out of his pond.

"There," said I, "he has got a fish."

"Well," said the old man, who was looking all the while, but could see nothing, "he did n't dive, he just wet his claws."

And, sure enough, he did not this time, though it is said that they often do, but he merely stooped low enough to pick him out with his talons; but as he bore his shining prey over the bushes, it fell to the ground, and we did not see that he recovered it. That is not their practice.

Thus, having had another crack with the old man, he standing bareheaded under the eaves, he directed us "athwart the fields," and we took to the beach again for another day, it being now late in the morning.

It was but a day or two after this that the safe of the Provincetown Bank was broken open and robbed by two men from the interior, and we learned that our hospitable entertainers did at least transiently harbor the suspicion that we were the men.

The Beach Again

To-DAY THE AIR was beautifully clear, and the sea no longer dark and stormy, though the waves still broke with foam along the beach, but sparkling and full of life. Already that morning I had seen the day break over the sea as if it came out of its bosom:—

> The saffron-robed Dawn rose in haste from
>   the streams
> Of Ocean, that she might bring light to
>   immortals and to mortals.

The sun rose visibly at such a distance over the sea, that the cloud-bank in the horizon, which at first concealed him, was not perceptible until he had risen high behind it, and plainly broke and dispersed it, like an arrow. But as yet I looked at him as rising over land, and could not, without an effort, realize that he was rising over the sea. Already I saw some vessels on the horizon, which had rounded the Cape in the night, and were now well on their watery way to other lands.

We struck the beach again in the south part of Truro. In the early part of the day, while it was flood tide, and the beach was narrow and soft, we walked

on the bank, which was very high here, but not so
level as the day before, being more interrupted by
slight hollows.

There were many vessels, like gulls, skimming
over the surface of the sea, now half concealed in its
troughs, their dolphin-strikers ploughing the water,
now tossed on the top of the billows. One, a barque
standing down parallel with the coast, suddenly
furled her sails, came to anchor, and swung round in
the wind, near us, only half a mile from the shore. At
first we thought that her captain wished to communicate with us, and perhaps we did not regard the
signal of distress, which a mariner would have understood, and he cursed us for cold-hearted wreckers
who turned our backs on him. For hours we could
still see her anchored there behind us, and we wondered how she could afford to loiter so long in her
course. Or was she a smuggler who had chosen that
wild beach to land her cargo on? Or did they wish to
catch fish, or paint their vessel? Erelong other banks,
and brigs, and schooners, which had in the mean
while doubled the Cape, sailed by her in the smack-
ing breeze, and our consciences were relieved. Some
of these vessels lagged behind, while others steadily
went ahead. We narrowly watched their rig and the
cut of their jibs, and how they walked the water, for
there was all the difference between them that there

is between living creatures. But we wondered that they should be remembering Boston and New York and Liverpool, steering for them, out there; as if the sailor might forget his peddling business on such a grand highway. They had perchance brought oranges from the Western Isles; and were they carrying back the peel? We might as well transport our old traps across the ocean of eternity. Is *that* but another "trading flood," with its blessed isles? Is Heaven such a harbor as the Liverpool docks?

As we were walking close to the water's edge this morning, we turned round, by chance, and saw a large black object which the waves had just cast up on the beach behind us, yet too far off for us to distinguish what it was; and when we were about to return to it, two men came running from the bank, where no human beings had appeared before, as if they had come out of the sand, in order to save it before another wave took it. As we approached, it took successively the form of a huge fish, a drowned man, a sail or a net, and finally of a mass of tow-cloth, part of the cargo of the Franklin, which the men loaded into a cart.

Objects on the beach, whether men or inanimate things, look not only exceedingly grotesque, but much larger and more wonderful than they actually are. Lately, when approaching the sea-shore several

degrees south of this, I saw before me, seemingly
half a mile distant, what appeared like bold and
rugged cliffs on the beach, fifteen feet high, and
whitened by the sun and waves; but after a few
steps it proved to be low heaps of rags—part of the
cargo of a wrecked vessel—scarcely more than a
foot in height. Once also it was my business to go in
search of the relics of a human body, mangled by
sharks, which had just been cast up, a week after a
wreck, having got the direction from a light-house: I
should find it a mile or two distant over the sand, a
dozen rods from the water, covered with a cloth, by
a stick stuck up. I expected that I must look very
narrowly to find so small an object, but the sandy
beach, half a mile wide, and stretching farther than
the eye could reach, was so perfectly smooth and
bare, and the mirage toward the sea so magnifying,
that when I was half a mile distant the insignificant
sliver which marked the spot looked like a bleached
spar, and the relics were as conspicuous as if they
lay in state on that sandy plain, or a generation had
labored to pile up their cairn there. Close at hand
they were simply some bones with a little flesh ad-
hering to them, in fact, only a slight inequality in the
sweep of the shore. There was nothing at all remarkable about them, and they were singularly inoffen-
sive both to the senses and the imagination. But as I
stood there they grew more and more imposing.

They were alone with the beach and the sea, whose hollow roar seemed addressed to them, and I was impressed as if there was an understanding between them and the ocean which necessarily left me out, with my snivelling sympathies. That dead body had taken possession of the shore, and reigned over it as no living one could, in the name of a certain majesty which belonged to it.

We afterward saw many small pieces of tow-cloth washed up, and I learn that it continued to be found in good condition, even as late as November in that year, half a dozen bolts at a time.

Sometimes we sat on the wet beach and watched the beach birds, sand-pipers, and others, trotting along close to each wave, and waiting for the sea to cast up their breakfast. The former (*Charadrius melodus*) ran with great rapidity and then stood stock still remarkably erect and hardly to be distinguished from the beach. The wet sand was covered with small skipping Sea Fleas, which apparently make a part of their food. These last are the little scavengers of the beach, and are so numerous that they will devour large fishes, which have been cast up, in a very short time. One little bird not larger than a sparrow,—it may have been a Phalarope,—would alight on the turbulent surface where the breakers were five or six feet high, and float buoyantly there like a duck, cunningly taking to its wings and lifting itself a few feet through the air over the foaming crest of each breaker, but sometimes outriding safely a considerable billow which hid it some seconds, when its instinct told it that it would not break. It was a little creature thus to sport with the ocean, but it was as perfect a success in its way as the breakers in theirs.

The sea, vast and wild as it is, bears thus the waste and wrecks of human art to its remotest shore. There is no telling what it may not vomit up. It lets nothing lie; not even the giant clams which cling to its bottom. It is still heaving up the tow-cloth of the Franklin, and perhaps a piece of some old pirate's ship, wrecked more than a hundred years ago, comes ashore to-day. Some years since, when a vessel was wrecked here which had nutmegs in her cargo, they were strewn all along the beach, and for a considerable time were not spoiled by the salt water. Soon afterward, a fisherman caught a cod which was full of them. Why, then, might not the Spice-Islanders shake their nutmeg-trees into the ocean, and let all nations who stand in need of them pick them up? However, after a year, I found that the nutmegs from the Franklin had become soft.

You might make a curious list of articles which fishes have swallowed,—sailors' open clasp-knives, and bright tin snuff-boxes, not knowing what was in them,—and jugs, and jewels, and Jonah. The other day I came across the following scrap in a newspaper.

A RELIGIOUS FISH.—A short time ago, mine host Stewart, of the Denton Hotel, purchased a rock-fish, weighing about sixty pounds. On opening it he found in it a certificate of membership of the M. E. Church, which we read as follows:—

<table>
<tr><td></td><td>Member</td></tr>
<tr><td>Methodist E. Church.</td><td></td></tr>
<tr><td>   Founded A. D. 1784.</td><td></td></tr>
<tr><td>Quarterly Ticket.</td><td>18</td></tr>
<tr><td></td><td>Minister.</td></tr>
</table>

"For our light affliction, which is but for a moment, worketh for us a far more exceeding *and* eternal weight of glory."

—2 Cor. iv. 17.

O what are all my sufferings here,
   If, Lord, thou count me meet
With that enraptured host t' appear,
   And worship at thy feet.

The paper was of course in a crumpled and wet condition, but on exposing it to the sun and ironing the kinks out of it, it became quite legible.   —*Denton (Md.) Journal.*

From time to time we sat under the lee of a sand-hill on the bank, thinly covered with coarse beach-grass, and steadily gazed on the sea, or watched the vessels going south, all Blessings of the Bay of course. We could see a little more than half a circle of ocean, besides the glimpses of the Bay which we got behind us; the sea there was not wild and dreary in all respects, for there were frequently a hundred sail in sight at once on the Atlantic. You can commonly count about eighty in a favorable summer day, and pilots sometimes land and ascend the bank to look out for those which require their services. These had been waiting for fair weather, and had come out of Boston Harbor together.

It was a poetic recreation to watch those distant sails steering for half fabulous ports, whose very names are a mysterious music to our ears: Fayal, and Babel-mandel, ay, and Chagres, and Panama,—bound to the famous Bay of San Francisco, and the golden streams of Sacramento and San Joaquin, to Feather River and the American Fork, where Sutter's Fort presides, and inland stands the City de los An-geles. It is remarkable that men do not sail the sea with more expectation. Nothing remarkable was ever accomplished in a prosaic mood. The heroes and dis-coverers have found true more than was previously believed, only when they were expecting and dreaming of something more than their contemporaries dreamed of, or even themselves discovered, that is, when they were in a frame of mind fitted to behold the truth. Referred to the world's standard, they are always insane.

Though there were numerous vessels at this great distance in the horizon on every side, yet the vast spaces between them, like the spaces between the stars, far as they were distant from us, so were they from one another—nay, some were twice as far from each other as from us,—impressed us with a sense of the immensity of the ocean, the "unfruitful ocean," as it has been called, and we could see what proportion man and his works bear to the globe. As we looked off, and saw the water growing darker and darker and deeper and deeper the farther we looked, till it was awful to consider, and it appeared to have no relation to the friendly land, either as shore or bottom,—of what use is a bottom if it is out of sight, if it is two or three miles from the surface, and you are to be drowned so long before you get to it, though it were made of the same stuff with your native soil?— over that ocean, where, as the Veda says, "there is nothing to give support, nothing to rest upon, nothing to cling to," I felt that I was a land animal. The man in a balloon even may commonly alight on the earth in a few moments, but the sailor's only hope is that he may reach the distant shore. I could then appreciate the heroism of the old navigator, Sir Humphrey Gilbert, of whom it is related, that being overtaken by a storm when on his return from America, in the year 1583, far northeastward from where we were, sitting abaft with a book in his hand, just before he was swallowed up in the deep, he cried out to his comrades in the Hind, as they came within hearing, "We are as near to Heaven by sea as by land." I saw that it would not be easy to realize.

On Cape Cod, the next most eastern land you hear of is St. George's Bank (the fishermen tell of "Georges," "Cashus," and other sunken lands which they frequent). Every Cape man has a theory about George's Bank having been an island once, and in their accounts they gradually reduce the shallowness from six, five, four, two fathoms, to somebody's confident assertion that he has seen a mackerel-gull sitting on a piece of dry land there. It reminded me, when I thought of the shipwrecks which had taken place there, of the Isle of Demons, laid down off this coast in old charts of the New World. There must be something monstrous, methinks, in a vision of the sea bottom from over some bank a thousand miles from the shore, more awful than its imagined bottomlessness; a drowned continent, all livid and frothing at the nostrils, like the body of a drowned man, which is better sunk deep than near the surface.

* * *

Yet this same placid Ocean, as civil now as a city's harbor, a place for ships and commerce, will erelong be lashed into sudden fury, and all its caves and cliffs will resound with tumult. It will ruthlessly heave these vessels to and fro, break them in pieces in its sandy or stony jaws, and deliver their crews to sea-monsters. It will play with them like sea-weed, distend them like dead frogs, and carry them about, now high, now low, to show to the fishes, giving them a nibble. This gentle Ocean will toss and tear the rag of a man's body like the father of mad bulls, and his relatives may be seen seeking the remnants for weeks along the strand. From some quiet inland hamlet they have rushed weeping to the unheard-of shore, and now stand uncertain where a sailor has recently been buried amid the sand-hills.

It is generally supposed that they who have long been conversant with the Ocean can foretell, by certain indications, such as its roar and the notes of sea-fowl, when it will change from calm to storm; but probably no such ancient mariner as we dream of exists; they know no more, at least, than the older sailors do about this voyage of life on which we are all embarked. Nevertheless, we love to hear the sayings of old sailors, and their accounts of natural phenomena, which totally ignore, and are ignored by, science; and possibly they have not always looked over the gunwale so long in vain. Kalm repeats a story which was told him in Philadelphia by a Mr. Cock, who was one day sailing to the West Indies in a small yacht, with an old man on board who was well acquainted with those seas. "The old man sounding the depth, called to the mate to tell Mr. Cock to launch the boats immediately, and to put a sufficient number of men into them, in order to tow the yacht during the calm, that they might reach the island before them as soon as possible, as within twenty-four hours there would be a strong hurricane. Mr. Cock asked him what reasons he had to think so; the old man replied, that on sounding, he saw the lead in the water at a distance of many fathoms more than he had seen it before; that therefore the water was become clear all of a sudden, which he looked upon as a certain sign of an impending hurricane in the sea." The sequel of the story is, that by good fortune, and by dint of rowing, they managed to gain a safe harbor before the hurricane had reached its height; but it finally raged with so much violence, that not only many ships were lost and houses unroofed, but even their own vessel in harbor was washed so far on shore that several weeks elapsed before it could be got off.

Though we have indulged in some placid reflections of late, the reader must not forget that the dash and roar of the waves were incessant. Indeed, it would be well if he were to read with a large conch-shell at his ear. But notwithstanding that it was very cold and windy to-day, it was such a cold as we thought would not cause one to take cold who was exposed to it, owing to the saltness of the air and the dryness of the soil.

The Sea and the Desert

THE CAPE became narrower and narrower as we approached its wrist between Truro and Provincetown, and the shore inclined more decidedly to the west. At the head of East Harbor Creek, the Atlantic is separated but by half a dozen rods of sand from the tide-waters of the Bay. From the Clay Pounds the bank flatted off for the last ten miles to the extremity at Race Point, though the highest parts, which are called "islands" from their appearance at a distance on the sea, were still seventy or eighty feet above the Atlantic, and afforded a good view of the latter, as well as constant view of the Bay, there being no trees nor a hill sufficient to interrupt it. Also the sands began to invade the land more and more, until finally they had entire possession from sea to sea, at the narrowest part. For three or four miles between Truro and Provincetown there were no inhabitants from shore to shore, and there were but three or four houses for twice that distance.

As we plodded along, either by the edge of the ocean, where the sand was rapidly drinking up the last wave that wet it, or over the sand-hills of the bank, the mackerel fleet continued to pour round the Cape north of us, ten or fifteen miles distant, in countless numbers, schooner after schooner, till they made a city on the water. They were so thick that many appeared to be afoul of one another; now all standing on this tack, now on that.

Still one after another the mackerel schooners hove in sight round the head of the Cape, "whitening all the sea road," and we watched each one for a moment with an undivided interest. It seemed a pretty sport. Here in the country it is only a few idle boys or loafers that go a-fishing on a rainy day; but there it appeared as if every able-bodied man and helpful boy in the Bay had gone out on a pleasure excursion in their yachts, and all would at last land and have a chowder on the Cape. The gazetteer tells you gravely how many of the men and boys of these towns are engaged in the whale, cod, and mackerel fishery, how many go to the banks of Newfoundland, or the coast of Labrador, the Straits of Belle Isle or the Bay of Chaleurs (Shalore the sailors call it); as if I were to reckon up the number of boys in Concord who are engaged during the summer in the perch, pickerel, bream, hornpout, and shiner fishery, of which no one keeps the statistics,—though I think that it is pursued with as much profit to the moral and intellectual man (or boy), and certainly with less danger to the physical one.

One of my playmates, who was apprenticed to a

printer, and was somewhat of a wag, asked his master one afternoon if he might go a-fishing, and his master consented. He was gone three months. When he came back, he said that he had been to the Grand Banks, and went to setting type again as if only an afternoon had intervened.

I confess I was surprised to find that so many men spent their whole day, ay, their whole lives almost, a-fishing. It is remarkable what a serious business men make of getting their dinners, and how universally shiftlessness and a grovelling taste take refuge in a merely ant-like industry. Better go without your dinner, I thought, than be thus everlastingly fishing for it like a cormorant. Of course, *viewed from the shore,* our pursuits in the country appear not a whit less frivolous.

I once sailed three miles on a mackerel cruise myself. It was a Sunday evening after a very warm day in which there had been frequent thunder-showers, and I had walked along the shore from Cohasset to Duxbury. I wished to get over from the last place to Clark's Island, but no boat could stir, they said, at that stage of the tide, they being left high on the mud. At length I learned that the tavern-keeper, Winsor, was going out mackerelling with seven men that evening, and would take me. When there had been due delay, we one after another straggled down to the shore in a leisurely manner, as if waiting for the tide still, and in India-rubber boots, or carrying

our shoes in our hands, waded to the boats, each of
the crew bearing an armful of wood, and one a
bucket of new potatoes besides. Then they resolved
that each should bring one more armful of wood, and
that would be enough. They had already got a barrel
of water, and had some more in the schooner. We
shoved the boats a dozen rods over the mud and
water till they floated, then rowing half a mile to the
vessel climbed aboard, and there we were in a mackerel schooner, a fine stout vessel of forty-three tons,
whose name I forget. The baits were not dry on the
hooks. There was the mill in which they ground
the mackerel, and the trough to hold it, and the long-
handled dipper to cast it overboard with; and already
in the harbor we saw the surface rippled with schools
of small mackerel, the real *Scomber vernalis*. The
crew proceeded leisurely to weigh anchor and raise
their two sails, there being a fair but very slight
wind;—and the sun now setting clear and shining on
the vessel after the thunder-showers, I thought that I
could not have commenced the voyage under more
favorable auspices. They had four dories and commonly fished in them, else they fished on the star-
board side aft where their lines hung ready, two to a
man. The boom swung round once or twice, and
Winsor cast overboard the foul juice of mackerel
mixed with rain-water which remained in his trough,
and then we gathered about the helmsman and told

stories. I remember that the compass was affected by
iron in its neighborhood and varied a few degrees.
There was one among us just returned from California, who was now going as passenger for his health
and amusement. They expected to be gone about a
week, to begin fishing the next morning, and to carry
their fish fresh to Boston. They landed me at Clark's
Island, where the Pilgrims landed, for my companions wished to get some milk for the voyage. But I
had seen the whole of it. The rest was only going to
sea and catching the mackerel. Moreover, it was as
well that I did not remain with them, considering the
small quantity of supplies they had taken.

Now I saw the mackerel fleet *on its fishing-ground,*
though I was not at first aware of it. So my experience was complete.

It was even more cold and windy to-day than
before, and we were frequently glad to take shelter
behind a sand-hill. None of the elements were resting. On the beach there is a ceaseless activity, always
something going on, in storm and in calm, winter
and summer, night and day. Even the sedentary man
here enjoys a breadth of view which is almost equiv-
alent to motion. In clear weather the laziest may look
across the Bay as far as Plymouth at a glance, or over
the Atlantic as far as human vision reaches, merely
raising his eyelids; or if he is too lazy to look after all,
he can hardly help *hearing* the ceaseless dash and

roar of the breakers. The restless ocean may at any moment cast up a whale or a wrecked vessel at your feet. All the reporters in the world, the most rapid stenographers, could not report the news it brings. No creature could move slowly where there was so much life around. The few wreckers were either going or coming, and the ships and the sand-pipers, and the screaming gulls overhead; nothing stood still but the shore. The little beach-birds trotted past close to the water's edge, or paused but an instant to swallow their food, keeping time with the elements.

The sea-shore is a sort of neutral ground, a most advantageous point from which to contemplate this world. It is even a trivial place. The waves forever rolling to the land are too far-travelled and untamable to be familiar. Creeping along the endless beach amid the sun-squawl and the foam, it occurs to us that we, too, are the product of sea-slime.

It is a wild, rank place, and there is no flattery in it. Strewn with crabs, horse-shoes, and razor-clams, and whatever the sea casts up,—a vast *morgue,* where famished dogs may range in packs, and crows come daily to glean the pittance which the tide leaves them. The carcasses of men and beasts together lie stately up upon its shelf, rotting and bleaching in the sun and waves, and each tide turns them in their beds, and tucks fresh sand under them. There is naked Nature,—inhumanly sincere, wasting no thought on man, nibbling at the cliffy shore where gulls wheel amid the spray.

Though once there were more whales cast up here, I think that it was never more wild than now. We do not associate the idea of antiquity with the ocean, nor wonder how it looked a thousand years ago, as we do of the land, for it was equally wild and unfathomable always. The Indians have left no traces on its surface, but it is the same to the civilized man and the savage. The aspect of the shore only has changed. The ocean is a wilderness reaching round the globe, wilder than a Bengal jungle, and fuller of monsters, washing the very wharves of our cities and the gardens of our sea-side residences. Serpents, bears, hyenas, tigers, rapidly vanish as civilization advances, but the most populous and civilized city cannot scare a shark far from its wharves. It is no further advanced than Singapore, with its tigers, in this respect. The Boston papers had never told me that there were seals in the harbor. I had always associated these with the Esquimaux and other outlandish people. Yet from the parlor windows all along the coast you may see families of them sporting on the flats. They were as strange to me as the merman would be. Ladies who never walk in the woods, sail over the sea. To go to sea! Why, it is to have the experience of Noah,—to realize the deluge. Every vessel is an ark.

* * *

After we had been walking many hours, the mackerel fleet still hovered in the northern horizon nearly in the same direction, but farther off, hull down. Though their sails were set they never sailed away, nor yet came to anchor, but stood on various tacks as close together as vessels in a haven, and we, in our ignorance, thought that they were contending patiently with adverse winds, beating eastward; but we learned afterward that they were even then on their fishing-ground, and that they caught mackerel without taking in their mainsails or coming to anchor, "a smart breeze" (thence called a mackerel breeze) being, as one says, "considered most favorable" for this purpose. We counted about two hundred sail of mackerel fishers within one small arc of the horizon, and a nearly equal number had disappeared southward. Thus they hovered about the extremity of the Cape, like moths round a candle; the lights at Race Point and Long Point being bright candles for them at night,—and at this distance they looked fair and white, as if they had not yet flown into the light, but nearer at hand afterward, we saw how some had formerly singed their wings and bodies.

A village seems thus, where its able-bodied men are all ploughing the ocean together, as a common field. In North Truro the women and girls may sit at their doors, and see where their husbands and brothers are harvesting their mackerel fifteen or twenty miles off, on the sea, with hundreds of white harvest wagons, just as in the country the farmers' wives sometimes see their husbands working in a distant hillside field. But the sound of no dinner-horn can reach the fisher's ear.

Having passed the narrowest part of the waist of the Cape, though still in Truro, for this township is about twelve miles long on the shore, we crossed over to the Bay side, not half a mile distant, in order to spend the noon on the nearest shrubby sand-hill in Provincetown, called Mount Ararat, which rises one hundred feet above the ocean. On our way thither we had occasion to admire the various beautiful forms and colors of the sand, and we noticed an interesting mirage, which I have since found that Hitchcock also observed on the sands of the Cape. We were crossing a shallow valley in the Desert, where the smooth and spotless sand sloped upward by a small angle to the horizon on every side, and at the lowest part was a long chain of clear but shallow pools. As we were approaching these for a drink in a diagonal direction across the valley, they appeared inclined at a slight but decided angle to the horizon, though they were plainly and broadly connected with one another, and there was not the least ripple to suggest a current; so that by the time we had reached a convenient part of one we seemed to have ascended several feet. They appeared to lie by magic on the side of the vale, like a mirror left in a slanting position. It was a very pretty mirage for a Province-town desert, but not amounting to what, in Sanscrit, is called "the thirst of the gazelle," as there was real water here for a base, and we were able to quench our thirst after all.

From the above-mentioned sand-hill we over-looked Provincetown and its harbor, now emptied of vessels, and also a wide expanse of ocean. As we did not wish to enter Provincetown before night, though it was cold and windy, we returned across the Deserts to the Atlantic side, and walked along the beach again nearly to Race Point, being still greedy of the sea in-fluence. All the while it was not so calm as the reader may suppose, but it was blow, blow, blow,—roar, roar, roar,—tramp, tramp, tramp,—without interruption. The shore now trended nearly east and west.

Before sunset, having already seen the mackerel fleet returning into the Bay, we left the sea-shore on the north of Provincetown, and made our way across the Desert to the eastern extremity of the town. From the first high sand-hill, covered with beach-grass and bushes to its top, on the edge of the desert, we overlooked the shrubby hill and swamp country which surrounds Provincetown on the north, and protects it, in some measure, from the invading sand. Notwithstanding the universal barrenness, and the contiguity of the desert, I never saw an autumnal landscape so beautifully painted as this was. It was like the richest rug imaginable spread over an uneven surface; no damask nor velvet, nor Tyrian dye or stuffs, nor the work of any loom, could ever match it. There was the incredibly bright red of the Huckle-berry, and the reddish brown of the Bayberry, min-gled with the bright and living green of small Pitch-Pines, and also the duller green of the Bayberry, Boxberry, and Plum, the yellowish green of the Shrub Oaks, and the various golden and yellow and fawn colored tints of the Birch and Maple and Aspen,— each making its own figure, and, in the midst, the few yellow sand-slides on the sides of the hills looked like the white floor seen through rents in the rug. Coming from the country as I did, and many autum-nal woods as I had seen, this was perhaps the most novel and remarkable sight that I saw on the Cape.

The next morning, though it was still more cold and blustering than the day before, we took to the Deserts again, for we spent our days wholly out of doors, in the sun when there was any, and in the wind which never failed. After threading the shrubby hill country at the southwest end of the town, west of the Shank-Painter Swamp, whose expressive name— for we understood it at first as a landsman naturally would—gave it importance in our eyes, we crossed the sands to the shore south of Race Point and three miles distant, and thence roamed round eastward through the desert to where we had left the sea the evening before. We travelled five or six miles after we got out there, on a curving line, and might have gone nine or ten, over vast platters of pure sand, from the midst of which we could not see a particle of vegetation, excepting the distant thin fields of Beach-grass, which crowned and made the ridges toward which the sand sloped upward on each side;—all the while in the face of a cutting wind as cold as January; indeed, we experienced no weather so cold as this for nearly two months afterward.

The attention of the general government was first attracted to the danger which threatened Cape Cod Harbor from the inroads of the sand, about thirty years ago, and commissioners were at that time appointed by Massachusetts to examine the premises. They reported in June, 1825, that, owing to "the trees and brush having been cut down, and the beach-grass destroyed on the seaward side of the Cape, opposite the Harbor," the original surface of the ground had been broken up and removed by the wind toward the Harbor,—during the previous fourteen years,—over an extent of "one half a mile in breadth, and about four and a half miles in length."—"The space where a few years since were some of the highest lands on the Cape, covered with trees and bushes," presenting "an extensive waste of undulating sand";—and that, during the previous twelve months, the sand "had approached the Harbor an average distance of fifty rods, for an extent of four and a half miles!" and unless some measures were adopted to check its progress, it would in a few years destroy both the harbor and the town. They therefore recommended that beach-grass be set out on a curving line over a space ten rods wide and four and a half miles long, and that cattle, horses, and sheep be prohibited from going abroad, and the inhabitants from cutting the brush.

I was told that about thirty thousand dollars in all had been appropriated to this object, though it was complained that a great part of it was spent foolishly, as the public money is wont to be. Some say that while the government is planting beach-grass behind the town for the protection of the harbor, the inhabitants are rolling the sand into the harbor in wheelbarrows, in order to make house-lots. The Patent-Office has recently imported the seed of this grass from Holland, and distributed it over the country, but probably we have as much as the Hollanders.

Thus Cape Cod is anchored to the heavens, as it were, by a myriad little cables of beach-grass, and, if they should fail, would become a total wreck, and erelong go to the bottom. Formerly, the cows were permitted to go at large, and they ate many strands of the cable by which the Cape is moored, and wellnigh set it adrift, as the bull did the boat which was moored with a grass rope; but now they are not permitted to wander.

* * *

The wind blowed so hard from the northeast, that, cold as it was, we resolved to see the breakers on the Atlantic side, whose din we had heard all the morning; so we kept on eastward through the Desert, till we struck the shore again north-east of Provincetown, and exposed ourselves to the full force of the piercing blast. There are extensive shoals there over which the sea broke with great force. For half a mile from the shore it was one mass of white breakers, which, with the wind, made such a din that we could hardly hear ourselves speak. Of this part of the coast it is said: "A northeast storm, the most violent and fatal to seamen, as it is frequently accompanied with snow, blows directly on the land: a strong current sets along the shore: add to which that ships, during the operation of such a storm, endeavor to work northward, that they may get into the bay. Should they be unable to weather Race Point, the wind drives them on the shore, and a shipwreck is inevitable. Accordingly, the strand is everywhere covered with the fragments of vessels." But since the Highland Light was erected, this part of the coast is less dangerous, and it is said that more shipwrecks occur south of that light, where they were scarcely known before.

This was the stormiest sea that we witnessed,— more *tumultuous,* my companion affirmed, than the rapids of Niagara, and, of course, on a far greater scale. It was the ocean in a gale, a clear, cold day, with only one sail in sight, which labored much, as if it were anxiously seeking a harbor. It was high tide when we reached the shore, and in one place, for a considerable distance, each wave dashed up so high that it was difficult to pass between it and the bank.

Having lingered on the shore till we were wellnigh chilled to death by the wind, and were ready to take shelter in a Charity-house, we turned our weather-beaten faces toward Provincetown and the Bay again, having now more than doubled the Cape.

SHAMBHALA LIBRARY

The Art of War: The Denma Translation, by Sun Tzu.
Translated by the Denma Translation Group.

The Art of Worldly Wisdom, by Baltasar Gracián.

Backwoods and along the Seashore: Selections from
The Maine Woods *and* Cape Cod, by Henry David
Thoreau. Edited by Peter Turner.

The Book of Five Rings, by Miyamoto Musashi.
Translated by Thomas Cleary.

The Book of Tea, by Kakuzo Okakura.

*The Erotic Spirit: An Anthology of Poems of Sensuality,
Love, and Longing,* edited by Sam Hamill.

I Ching: The Book of Change, by Cheng Yi.
Translated by Thomas Cleary.

Love Poems from the Japanese, translated by Kenneth
Rexroth. Edited by Sam Hamill.

Meditation in Action, by Chögyam Trungpa.

Nature and Other Writings, by Ralph Waldo Emerson.
Edited by Peter Turner.

New Seeds of Contemplation, by Thomas Merton.

The Poetry of Zen, edited and translated by Sam Hamill and J. P. Seaton.

The Sabbath: Its Meaning for Modern Man, by Abraham Joshua Heschel.

Shambhala: The Sacred Path of the Warrior, by Chögyam Trungpa. Edited by Carolyn Rose Gimian.

Siddhartha: A New Translation, by Hermann Hesse. Translated by Sherab Chödzin Kohn.

Start Where You Are: A Guide to Compassionate Living, by Pema Chödrön.

Tao Teh Ching, by Lao Tzu. Translated by John C. H. Wu.

Teachings of the Buddha, edited by Jack Kornfield.

The Tibetan Book of the Dead: The Great Liberation through Hearing in the Bardo, translated with commentary by Francesca Fremantle and Chögyam Trungpa.

The Way of Chuang Tzu, by Thomas Merton.

The Wisdom of the Desert: Sayings from the Desert Fathers of the Fourth Century, by Thomas Merton.

When Things Fall Apart: Heart Advice for Difficult Times, by Pema Chödrön.